MUSIC INDUSTRY FORMS

THE **75** MOST IMPORTANT DOCUMENTS FOR THE MODERN MUSICIAN

JONATHAN FEIST

Berklee Press

Editor in Chief: Jonathan Feist
Vice President of Online Learning and Continuing Education: Debbie Cavalier
Assistant Vice President of Operations for Berklee Media: Robert F. Green
Assistant Vice President of Marketing and Recruitment for Berklee Media: Mike King
Dean of Continuing Education: Carin Nuernberg
Editorial Assistants: Matthew Dunkle, Reilly Garrett, Zoë Lustri, José Rodrigo Vazquez

Front Cover Design: Sumit Shringi
Front Cover Photos: "Stage in Lights" Copyright Narcis Parfenti/Shutterstock.com; "Clipboard" by Rangizz/Shutterstock.com
Author Photo, About the Author: Patricia Gandolfo Mann
Author Photo, Back Cover: Wendy Parr, www.wendyparr.com

ISBN 978-0-87639-147-1

Study with
■ BERKLEE ONLINE

online.berklee.edu

DISTRIBUTED BY

HAL•LEONARD®
CORPORATION
7777 W. BLUEMOUND RD. P.O. BOX 13819
MILWAUKEE, WISCONSIN 53213

Visit Hal Leonard Online at
www.halleonard.com

CONTENTS

ACKNOWLEDGMENTS

Many people touched this book, directly and indirectly. Special thanks to Jeff Schroedl, Carin Nuernberg, Debbie Cavalier, Don Gorder, and the Berklee College of Music Educational Review Committee for their support of this concept and input into content. Thanks also to Jackie Muth and the staff at Hal Leonard Corp. (freelancers, too) for the many dimensions of magic they work on this and all Berklee Press books. And a huge shout-out to my Berklee Press editorial assistants, Matthew Dunkle, Reilly Garrett, Zoë Lustri, and José Rodrigo Vázquez always good sports, no matter what windmills I send them tilting after.

A number of individuals and organizations graciously shared their experiences and thoughts regarding content, and provided indispensable examples and models, particularly Shane Adams, Debbie Cavalier, Mark Cross, From the Top, Hal Leonard Corp., Mike King, superhero editor Susan Lindsay, Isaac Ho, David Patterson, Lalo Schifrin, Jeff Schroedl, Charys Schuler, Sean Slade, Peter Spellman, Don Teesdale, and Jonathan Adam Wyner. Special thanks to photographers Patricia Gandolfo Mann and Wendy Parr, for the author photos.

For endless anecdotes, war stories, and industry insights, I am very grateful to my authors, colleagues, and students at Berklee College of Music and Berklee Press, both on campus and from all around the world, via our online school. More recently, my friends at VocalizeU are continually providing new inspirations and insights.

And my most profound thanks goes to my family: my education reformer/ visionary wife Marci Cornell-Feist, amazing/hilarious sons Merlin and Forrest, and Cricket "the love beagle," who snuggles close or wags her tail just when it is needed the most.

I don't know how anyone could possibly write a book without them all.

INTRODUCTION. FORMS: FRIENDS OR FOES?

Like many musicians, I have long loathed inane bureaucracy. Forms often seem like perfunctory red tape blocking the path between well-meaning people and their ability to do good work.

But in 2002, outside my work at Berklee College of Music, I started participating in my small town's local government, serving on a few boards and eventually chairing the Town of Harvard Historical Commission (HHC). Suddenly, the tables turned. I found that my ability to preserve my town's beautiful old buildings was at the mercy of how well people filled out forms. And some of these forms were just dreadful. They were photocopies of photocopies of photocopies of ill-conceived typewritten forms created thirty years previously, sometimes supporting laws that had since changed.

One of my early revolutions was to update the HHC's standard application form for modifying protected historic properties. We considered what information was crucial, redesigned the form graphically so that there was actually room to enter the data that we were requesting, added some instructions on the back, and made a few other improvements. Lo and behold, we found that with this improved method of data collection, it became easier for us to achieve higher quality processes and decisions because our data was more complete and because the improved, clearer form encouraged better thinking and conversation about our applicants' proposed schemes.

My newfound zeal for bureaucracy spread to my work here in the music book/video publishing industry, and I began to take a closer look at the processes at work in my office. One of the early forms I developed was the CD Master Checklist, which has since helped us control some recurring issues in the audio masters used for our books, avoiding some potentially costly mistakes. Years and years later, it remains a really helpful tool.

Rather than pointless red tape, I have come to see *thoughtfully crafted* forms as a kind of checklist, designed to help everyone remember critical considerations and maintain quality control. Good forms can improve communication, save time, reduce risk, and encourage high quality results. I began to see the forms I come across in the music industry in a new light. Also, I realized that many of the books we've been working on, here at Berklee Press, discuss the critical forms used in music making: spotting notes, input lists, marketing one-sheets, and so many others. Clearly, music professionals have a tradition of valuing this kind of documentation. That said, in conversations I've had with wistful industry old-timers, it is clear that many standard music industry forms have been fading from use, despite their usefulness.

One theory about why some good forms are receding is that many musicians are now working in a more independent-operator business model, rather than as part of a larger corporate one. As a result, some clever tools that were long a part of industry culture (such as take sheets) are becoming relatively obscure. Younger generations of musicians are often less exposed to the institutional memory that kept the industry running for so many decades, and nobody explains some of the tools and conventions that were developed to solve common organizational problems. For instance, stage plots have certain symbology and conventions that may confuse the uninitiated, but that truly make life easier for both musicians and stage crew, once the hieroglyphics become clear. And that is the ultimate goal of this book: to present some tools that can make your life creating music easier.

My vantage point at Berklee gives me the opportunity to talk with an extraordinary number of seasoned music industry veterans about their work at a very specific nuts-and-bolts level. In working on their books, I get to ask them detailed, technical questions—okay, to geek out—in the normal course of conversation. Brilliant people come from all over the world to teach here, and so there's a kind of warehouse here of institutional memory from many different places (Hollywood, Nashville, New York, London, rural Maine...) that has informed this book at a profound level. While I personally have never engineered a session with James Brown, toured with Stan Getz, won a GRAMMY®, scored a Hollywood blockbuster, signed recording contracts with Billboard-charting artists, or auditioned thousands of performers hoping to win scholarships, I have been fortunate to edit books by people who have done all these things, and more. So, my task in this project has been to leap between shoulders of the many giants who surround me, and present some of the lessons they have shared.

Some forms discussed in this book, such as stage plots, are so critical and so relevant that you might use them every day. Many, such as gain stage diagrams, are long-established classics in the industry, and you can probably find tens of thousands of examples of their use in the field. Especially for old workhorse forms like those, I've included some of the abbreviations and symbols common to those contexts. Sometimes, I present a couple of variations.

A few forms are a little obscure. Non-engineers might be unlikely ever to draw up an audio archive reel sheet. However, understanding the recording archival shorthand used for so many decades can mean (and has meant) the difference between your reissuing a carefully engineered master or accidentally publishing a rough backup only intended as a safety copy.

An occasional form here should strike you as common sense. Repertoire lists (the songs your band is ready to play), for example, don't require unusual genius to invent. But I include them because they are standard and critical, and seeing them here might remind you that you need them, somewhere. Of course, you should have a repertoire list on your wedding band's website, silly! All the other wedding bands have them, and yours should too.

Some forms are also frequently used in other industries. For example, a "design spec" is common wherever graphical design is used, such as publishing and advertising. Musicians also manage a lot of graphical art creation these days: album art, Web page design, promo photography, and so on. Similarly, some of the classic project management forms aren't commonplace in the music industry yet, but I find them useful, and as I've been teaching *Project Management for Musicians* classes and workshops lately, maybe some others will start catching on.

Please keep in mind that these samples are not intended as "standard" or "gospel" for you to use verbatim. Rather, they are designed as starting points to spark your imagination of how similar tools can support your own work. You'll find regional and cultural variations of many of these details, even on the most common forms. *Vive la difference!* Hopefully, this presentation will give you the essential concept of how they can help, and perhaps decipher some confusing argot.

PART I

At the Gig

The forms in this section are common in performance settings, from bar rooms to concert halls to circus tents. Some are used by performing musicians, but they might also be prepared by stage managers, producers, sound engineers, and others involved in the show. Many have their origins in the theater.

1. STAGE PLOT

Stage plots (or *stage setup diagrams*) show the positions of music stands, chairs, and other equipment on a stage, ready for a rehearsal, performance, or recording. These diagrams are often prepared by the stage manager (informed by the artist), and are referenced by the stagehands. Touring artists frequently travel with their own stage plots. If the diagrams are sensibly drawn, they are generally received cheerfully by the local stage crew. Text helps clarify less common instruments or gear, designates major instrument sections, and distinguishes between specific risers (often, indicated in inches, such as 8" for eight-inch high risers) or the conductor's podium. Symbol legends are also a good idea, once you get beyond chairs and stands.

It is important to indicate the orientation of the diagram with relation to the audience. Towards that end, a rough approximation of the stage shape might be given, or a curvy/dotted line indicating the curtain/proscenium. A cross shape indicates center stage, and there might be an actual cross or X on the floor (a "spike") made with tape.

Stage directions describe the general stage geography. *Stage right* or *stage left* are the performer's right and left as they face the audience, as opposed to *house* or *camera* right and left, which is the audience perspective. Stage right and house left are the same place. *Downstage* is towards the audience; *upstage* is towards the back of the stage. When you "upstage" another performer, you approach them from behind and force them to turn away from the audience towards you, thus yielding their prominence. Actors have to worry about this more than musicians do.

Common symbols and terms:

X	chair
–	music stand
(piano symbol)	piano with bench
(harpsichord symbol)	harpsichord
□	podium or other risers, often accompanied by height indication
○	a drum, particularly tympani
•	upright bass stool
∿	curtain
-------------	proscenium ("in front of the scenery")
∪	audience chair
┼ or C:	center stage
U:	upstage
D:	downstage
DR or DSR/DL or DSL:	downstage right/left
UR or USR/UL or USL:	upstage right/left
DCR/DCL:	downstage, in the middle between center and right/left
UCR/UCL:	upstage, in the middle between center and right/left
FOH:	front of house (the audience, or where a sound engineer is sited in the audience)

Figure 1.1 shows a setup for a duet, where each player has one chair and two music stands. Their chairs are oriented so that they are facing diagonally, thus allowing good eye contact with each other, but also good interaction with the audience.

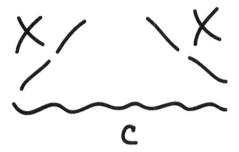

FIG. 1.1. Stage Plot for Duet

Figure 1.2 is for a quintet. Note that the pianist has both a piano bench and an extra chair, likely for a page-turner, who sits upstage and is thus fairly obscured from the audience's view. An upright bass player has a stool between the piano and drums. The drums are on a 4-inch riser. In this case, it is understood that the drummer will set up his instruments—often the case for a drum set, so it is not necessary to indicate every detail. Farthest downstage, two other musicians sit facing each other. The cross on the floor helps the stage crew center the setup symmetrically.

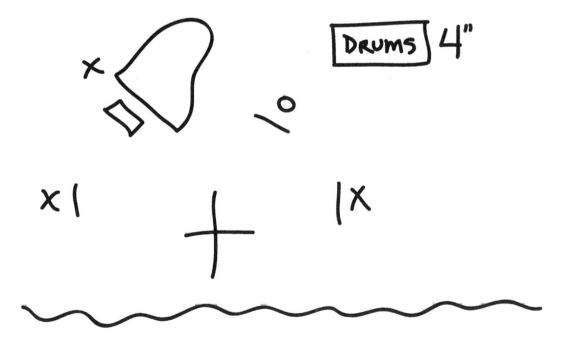

FIG. 1.2. Quintet

Figure 1.3 shows a setup diagram for an orchestra on a film scoring stage. This diagram uses the symbol [M] for a monitor, and it has a key in the lower right-hand corner, clarifying some details (including totals of chairs and stands). Instrument section names help clarify the complexity—particularly useful when an orchestra librarian uses the diagram and needs to know what parts go on what music stands. Note that in string sections, players often share stands. Also notice that everyone is angled to be able to see the conductor.

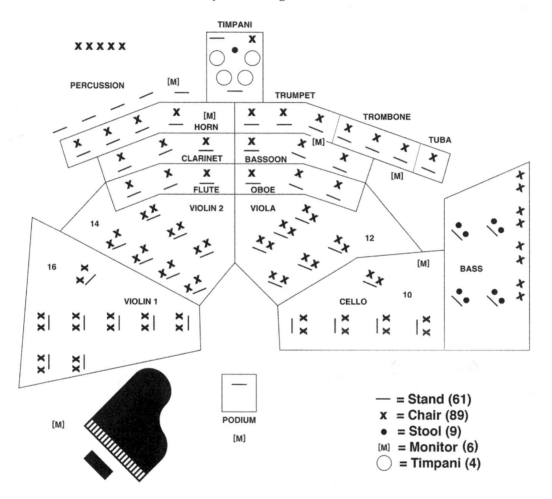

FIG. 1.3. Film Scoring Sound Stage

Concert Hall Layout

Here's a general layout of a concert hall, with common abbreviations. The *stage* is for the performers; the *house* is for the audience. The *backstage* area is invisible to the audience. The *wings* are part of the backstage area immediately off the stage, where performers "wait in the wings" to go on, hidden from the audience's view. This diagram shows one row of audience chairs. The *green room* is a longer-term holding/preparation/lounge area for performers waiting to go onstage. Some theaters have multiple green rooms; some have just one small private one for a small number of performers; some have enormous green rooms, theoretically sufficient to keep an entire waiting orchestra out of trouble. (Good luck with that.) The *prop room* is a live storage/ staging area for props, large instruments, scenery, or other equipment that comes on and off stage during a performance. Up above a theater's stage, not shown on this diagram, might be a *fly gallery*, where scenery can be manipulated via ropes and pulleys, and various *catwalks*, generally used for hanging/accessing lighting and sound equipment. There might also be dressing rooms, costume rooms, and so on.

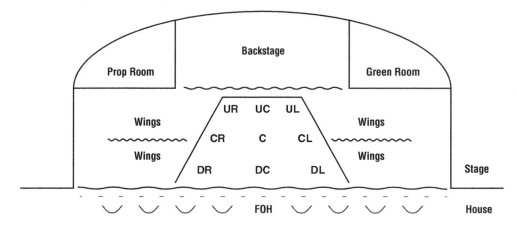

FIG. 1.4. Concert Hall Layout

2. SOUND PLOT AND INPUT LIST

Similar to a stage plot is a *sound plot*, sometimes called an "audio plot" or "live sound diagram." These diagrams indicate microphones and sometimes other audio gear, such as monitors and on-stage amplifiers. Numerals indicate the mic's channel through the mixing board, sometimes with arrows to indicate the directions in which they point. The accompanying microphone *input list* provides more detailed information regarding the specific microphone types, and may also specify preamps (more common in recording), pickup patterns, and other details.

Figure 2 is a sound plot for the quintet shown in figure 1.2. The piano has an indication "medium stick," indicating how high the piano's lid should be open. Besides the mics for the musicians, an additional lavaliere (lav) mic is indicated downstage left for an announcer. There are four monitor speakers, labeled M1 to M4. This diagram uses "DSC" as the stage direction orientation label: downstage center.

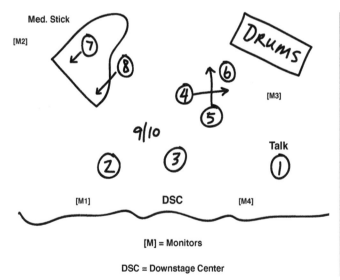

Channel	Description	Mic
1	Narrator	DPA-4060 (Lav)
2	Guitar	Shure SM57
3	T. Sax	KSM 32
4	Drums OHL	Fat Head II
5	Drums OHR	Fat Head II
6	Kick Drum	Shure Beta 52
7	Piano L	Shure KSM32
8	Piano R	Shure KSM32
9	Ac. Bass	AKG D12
10	Ac. Bass	Active DI Box

[M] = Monitors

DSC = Downstage Center

FIG. 2. Sound Plot with Input List

3. PERFORMANCE RUN SHEET

A performance *run sheet* (or "shift plot" or "cue sheet") is used by a stage manager to track all setup, scene, sound, and lighting changes that occur during the performance. Though these are also sometimes called "cue sheets," that's potentially confusing, because in the film/TV industry, "music cue sheets" (see form 25) refers to forms required by the performance rights organizations to help route broadcast royalties.

Each line of a run sheet is a *cue*—a component of the performance, or an order barked regarding that component. The cue might be a performance, an announcement, a video being shown, an intermission—any component. Indications are provided regarding lighting, stage setup, and so on. In figure 3, a run sheet shows the first half of a concert. *Estimated Timing* helps the stage manager keep the schedule on track and gives the audio engineer insight into what to expect. The *Description* column indicates what the audience perceives. *Cue* indicates a direction that the stage manager gives to someone, such as informing the sound engineer that a mic should go live. *Move* describes performer location changes onstage. *Notes* is for stage crew directions, and also who should be ready and "standing by," waiting in the wings to go on.

Some common terms:

Strike:	Remove from the stage, or more extremely, to completely disassemble a set.
Kill:	Turn something off (or remove from the stage, like "strike").
Up:	Lights go on.
Place or Set:	Put something somewhere.
"Places" (shouted):	Call for performers to take position onstage before the audience sees them.
X:	Symbol indicating the performer moves or crosses the stage.
Spike:	Temporary mark on the floor (often gaffer's tape) where something goes.
Reset:	Move it back neatly where it is supposed to go (after performer might have moved it).
Check:	Confirm that something has happened.
SM:	Stage manager.
CREW:	Stage crew. Individual names are assigned to each task. Some run sheets have a column for each member of the crew, showing exactly who does what. This clarifies complex maneuvers and facilitates last-minute crew personnel changes.

Run Sheet

Est. Timing	Description	Cue	Move	Notes
Preshow	Preset "Setup 1"			Piano to quarter stick, no music desk
0:00:00	Warning bell/Places			SM: QUARTET confirms ready DAVE: Check Wendy's Guild guitar tuning
0:07:00	House to Half; Places			SM: QUARTET standing by, Shane at Mic 10 SUE: Ready Fog Machine
0:09:30	House Out			SUE: Fog Machine On
0:10:00	"Intro" (SHANE)	SHANE to mic 10; Stage Lights Up, Shane X to stool	End: SHANE exits SL; QUARTET enters	SUE: Kill Fog Machine
0:10:30	"Baby Bat Blues" (QUARTET)			WENDY standing by
0:15:30	Quick tuning check (QUARTET)		Start: Shane X seat	DAVE: Set Wendy's Guild and stand at blue spike SUE: Strikes stool and stand
0:16:00	"Notebooks" (QUARTET and WENDY)		Start: WENDY enters	
0:24:30	"Intro to Missing Mattress" (RICH)	RICH to mic 10	End: RICH sits back down	DAVE: Reset Guild and stand at blue spike
0:25:30	"Missing Mattress" (QUARTET and WENDY)		End: WENDY exits SL	
0:34:00	"Intro to 'Water Torture'" (MIKE)	MIKE at mic 10		DAVE: Strike Guild/stand
0:36:00	"Water Torture" (QUARTET)		End: QUARTET exits SL	
0:45:30	House Up/Stage Lights Out			
0:45:30	Intermission: 15 minutes			CREW Strike piano/bench, set "Setup 2"

FIG. 3. Run Sheet for Performance (First Half)

4. SET LIST

A *set list* indicates the songs and their order during a *set*—an uninterrupted sequence of songs performed at a concert or gig. It's useful for the band, for the client, for the audience, and also, for administrative purposes after the event. Posted backstage, performers who don't play every piece can gauge whether there's time to hit the restroom, get some fresh air, and/or tune before they go onstage, or whether they must prioritize.

While most *programs* (i.e., the list of all songs performed) are decided in advance of the event (perhaps listed on a printed "program" for the audience), some set lists are decided on the fly, without being announced first. For particularly seasoned artists who are comfortable deciding what to play spontaneously, an ad hoc set list might be scrawled and distributed informally, right before the curtain goes up, or even recorded while the concert is underway. Either way, the list of what is performed must be documented and ultimately provided to the performance rights organizations, so that compensation can be administered to the music's copyright holders (see "Music Cue Sheet," form 25).

Besides the song title, a set list shared among musicians might also indicate the key, duration, and other notes about the arrangement. The set list in figure 4 shows two sets for a concert. One planned encore, "Immortality," is listed under the line of the second set.

Set 1	Set 2
1. The Moment I Found You (4:04)	1. Closet Demon (3:06)
2. Is Anybody Home at Home (5:25)	2. Here (2:51)
3. Our Place (3:55)	3. Someone Else's Blues (3:28)
4. You and Only You (2:45)	4. No Time (2:11)
5. Printed Wildflowers (2:45)	5. Crabby Day (2:32)
	6. Immortality (3:01)

FIG. 4. Set List. Courtesy of Fantasy Monologue.

5. SONG ORDER WORKSHEET

A *song order worksheet* helps chart out the essential information about songs, in preparation for a set list or album. This one includes philosophical guidelines about how to choose the song order.

Name	Key	Meter	Density	Mood
Is Anybody Home at Home	C major	4/4 at 68	Band, no drums	Pensive
The Moment I Found You	A♭ major	3/4 at 160	Band (biggest)	Happy
Our Place	A major	4/4 at 120 (8th feel)	Band	Happy
You and Only You	C major	4/4 at 92	Duo	Happy, ironic
Printed Wildflowers	C major	4/4 at 88	Moderate band	Sad
Closet Demon	D major	4/4 at 118	Big	Bitter, intense
Here	C minor	4/4 at 68	Band, no drums	Saddest
Someone Else's Blues	A minor	4/4 at 112; 8th	Duo	Ironic
No Time	C major	3/4 at 84	Quartet	Reflective, nostalgic
Crabby Day	C major	4/4 at 92	Band, no drums	Happy
Immortality	C major	4/4 at 72	Duo	Optimistic
• Avoid more than two adjacent songs in the same key or meter, or more than one with tempos under 70 bpm.				

FIG. 5. Song Order Worksheet

6. PERFORMER BREAKDOWN

A *performer breakdown* chart shows who is participating in a given piece of music. Performers reference it to see when they should be onstage, stage managers to confirm that the performers are ready, producers to schedule recording sessions efficiently, and it is also used by others. This version of the chart also shows instrument changes (for Wendy's two guitars).

Musician	Intro	"Baby Bat Blues"	Intro "Notebooks"	"Notebooks"	Intro "Missing Mattresses"	Missing Mattresses	Intro "Water Torture"	"Water Torture"
Shane —Keyboard	•	•		•		•		•
Rich —Guitar		•	•	•		•		•
Mike —Drums		•		•		•	•	•
Dave —Bass		•		•		•		•
Wendy —Fender Guitar				•	•			
—Guild Guitar						•		

FIG. 6. Performer Breakdown

7. PERFORMANCE REPORT

A *performance report* is usually generated by a stage manager or producer while a performance progresses, and used to track what transpires. The major sections are for timing notes and for tracking issues that will require discussion, repair/maintenance, procedure changes, performance issues, and so on. Variations of this form are used for rehearsals, usually with more feedback about the music (with piece by piece breakdowns) and less about tech (i.e., sound and lighting).

Event Name: Venue:			Date: Performance Duration:		
Setup	**House Opens**	**First Half**	**Intermission**	**Second Half**	**Strike**
Start:	Start:	Start:	Start:	Start:	Start:
Stop:		Stop:	Stop:	Stop:	Stop:
Total:		Total:	Total:	Total:	Total:
Performance Notes			Technical Notes		
House Notes			Building Notes		

FIG. 7. Performance Report

PART II

In the Studio

Forms in the recording studio help track the many hardware, software, and media assets involved in a music project. They are often generated by audio engineers and producers.

8. MIC ASSIGNMENT CHART

A *microphone assignment chart* (or "setup sheet," and similar to an "input list") lists the microphones, preamplifiers, and other information about how a track was recorded. Precisely documenting how the recording was made makes it easier to achieve consistency when you modify tracks, record overdub corrections, or create alternate versions, such as radio mixes or alternate lyric versions, long after the songs were originally recorded.

Mic Assignment List

Artist: Fantasy Monologue   **Date:** June 20, 2013

Track: "Baby Bat Blues"

Studio: King George Studios, Studio A   **Console:** API Legacy

Input	Track Name	Mic	Preamp	Notes
1	Main R	Earthworks M-30 (Omni)		
2	Main L	Earthworks M-30 (Omni)		
3	A. Guitar	U67		Martin
4	T. Sax	Royer R-121		
5	Drums OHL	AKG 414	Hardy M-1	
6	Drums OHR	AKG 414	Hardy M-1	
7	Kick Drum	AKG D112		
8	Snare (Top)	Shure SM57		
9	Snare (Bottom)	MD 441		
10	Hi-Hat	KM84		
11	Ride	KM84		
12	Rack Tom	MD 421		
13	Rack Tom	MD 421		
14	Floor Tom	AKG R20		
15	Piano R	AKG 451		Low Stick
16	Piano L	AKG 451		Low Stick
17	Upright Bass	Beyer M160	API 512c	
18	Lead Vocals	Neumann U47	Neve 1073	Pop Filter
19	BG Vocals 1	Neumann U87		Pop Filter
20	BG Vocals 2	Neumann U87		Pop Filter

FIG. 8. Mic Assignment Chart

9. RECALL SHEET

A *recall sheet* is a diagram of the settings on an individual piece of analog gear. The goal here is to document the settings used in a given recording. It shows every knob and switch that might get set during a session. In digital gear or plug-ins, this information is often savable with the project. You might also save a reusable "snapshot," "template," or "preset" of settings that can be transported into other projects. For analog gear, though, it is handy to make up a document for each piece of equipment, and then customize it to your specific session.

Here's a recall sheet for a Big Muff Pi, the classic guitar effects pedal with three controls: volume, tone, and sustain. At the top of the form, you indicate where these settings were used. Then in the diagram, a circle with ticks represents each Big Muff knob. Lines are then drawn in to document how each knob was set. For a simple gadget like the Big Muff, it's easy enough to just scribble out a diagram like this on the fly. For gear with more controls, though, it becomes a more important time-saver to draw up a blank recall sheet in advance so that during the session, you only have to draw in the settings. (Alternatively, snap a photo with your phone, and then include that photo on a form with the other information.)

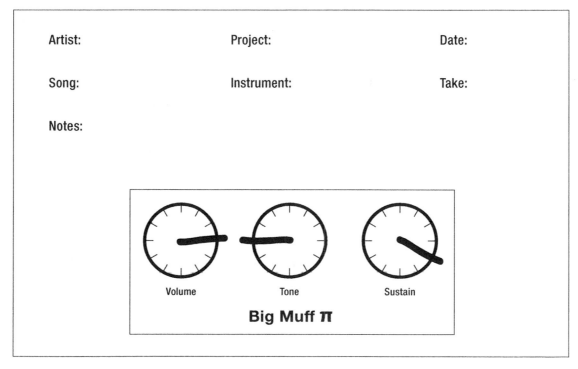

FIG. 9. Recall Sheet for a Big Muff π.

10. SIGNAL FLOW/GAIN STAGE DIAGRAM

A *signal flow diagram* is a simplified view of a recording setup, showing every device being used and arrows indicating the direction of signal flow. This type of "block diagram" is somewhere between an *audio plot* (showing physical stage setup) and an *audio schematic* (showing just the technology). So, the flow might start with an electric guitar, go through a series of effects pedals, then out of an amplifier, into a microphone, through a preamplifier, into a recording console, out to an outboard compressor, back to the console, through a reverb plug-in, and then out of the speakers. By charting it all out, an engineer can see all the factors that go into affecting the sound. This is helpful for trouble-shooting issues such as no sound, signal distortion, unwanted sound modi-fiers, and so on.

In figure 10, we can see that there are two signal chains for the guitar: one through an amp and microphone, and the other through a DI box. We can also see that there are two reverb ("verb") modification points. By methodi-cally mapping out what's modifying the sound, an engineer can gain greater control over the sound. In this case, for example, if there's too much reverb, the engineer can see that the guitarist is adding additional 'verb to the mix via the pedal. That might not be obvious to an engineer just eyeballing the situation through the control room window.

A simplified type of signal flow diagram is the *gain stage diagram*. These only indicate the points where "gain" (volume level) can be affected throughout the signal chain. Gain is controllable by many different devices: instruments, effects, preamplifiers, software plug-ins, and multiple locations within a console or DAW. So, a direct injection box might be included in a signal flow diagram but not a gain stage diagram, as DI boxes don't usually have gain controls. The diagram might begin/end with a microphone or other device that doesn't have a gain stage, just as a starting/ending point of the flow.

Traditionally, signal flow diagrams are read from left to right, top to bottom, with arrows indicating the direction of signal flow. Not all diagrams follow these standards, though, particularly when they reflect the physical layout of gear in a room. Items might be represented by pictures instead of simple rect-angles; these make the diagram friendlier, and perhaps, easier to interpret at a glance, but they are not necessary and require extra preparation time that might not be warranted. Circles sometimes indicate the start and end points of the chain. "In" means towards the device receiving a signal (such as a console); "out" means away from it.

Audio Schematics

Many of these conventions come from *audio schematics*, a more technical type of diagram used by electrical engineers, often featured in audio equipment manuals to show the inner workings of a device. Those have many more specific symbols, such as for resistors, capacitors, power sources, and so on—fascinating to be sure, but beyond our current scope. There is a kinship between the two diagramming styles, though.

Here, is a signal flow diagram set up to A/B a guitar track with and without the console's reverb.

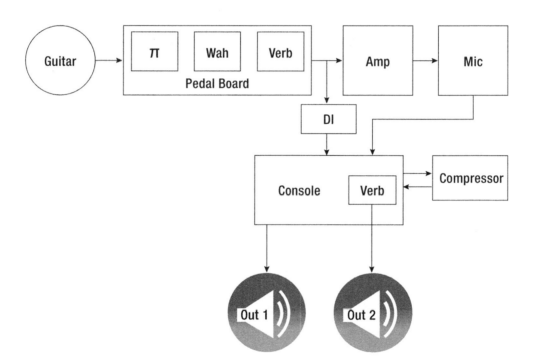

FIG. 10. Signal Flow Diagram

11. GEAR MAINTENANCE SCHEDULE

Some equipment and facilities require regular attention. Pianos need to be tuned, guitar strings need to be swapped out, batteries need to be changed. This chart will help you track and predict these necessities, which can help you keep up with the maintenance and avoid emergencies. Use it in conjunction with a calendar, ideally with automated reminders set well in advance of a needed repair. Some complicated gear or facilities might warrant an individual checklist of multiple things to do (such as the Stage Cleanup Checklist in form 12), but you might list the item once on this form and mention an attachment (such as with "Stage" in this form). When you do the service, check the Interval and reset the Next Service date.

Item	Service Needed	Who Does It	Service Duration	Cost	Warranty Expires	Interval	Next Service
Steinway Grand Piano	Tuning	Atherton Tuning	2 hours	$85	N/A	6 months, or before each concert	12/4/2014
Humidifier	Filter cleaning	Me	30 minutes	n/a	11/10/2015	12 months	8/15/2014
Boss Bass Pedal	Battery	Me	10 minutes	$2	N/A	3 months	10/16/2014
Septic System	Flushing	Cool Breeze Septic and Well	2 hours	$150	N/A	2 years	12/21/2014
Stage	**See attached**	Stage hands	1 hour	n/a	N/A	After every use	8/2/2013
Strobe	Replace bulb	Me	10 minutes	$15	N/A	2 years	2/1/2014
DX-1002	Factory tune-up	Manufacturer	3 weeks	$150	9/28/2018	3 years	3/3/2015

FIG. 11. Gear Maintenance Schedule

12. MAINTENANCE CHECKLIST

A *maintenance checklist* is helpful when an item or a room requires multiple actions. If you are trying to buckle down and make sure tasks get completed, you can require the person charged with completing this list to date and sign the form. That can make them take each item more seriously.

Stage Cleanup Checklist
Fold chairs and stack onto dollies.
Tighten loose music stands.
Stack music stands backstage.
Cover and lock Steinway.
Sweep stage/remove all trash.
Turn off lights.
Lock prop room door.
Open curtain.
Report unusual damage or circumstances on the back of this form.

FIG. 12. Stage Cleanup Checklist

13. ARTIST ARCHIVE INDEX

An *artist archive index* lists all assets related to a given artist or client. Sheets like this are maintained by individual artists, recording studios, organizations that organize the works of artists, and others who are trying to track a large amount of materials. Various code numbers uniquely identify each asset and are cross-referenced to additional pages and objects with more information. In figure 13, the "Cat. #" identifies the project, the "DAT #" identifies the storage unit, and the "ID #" identifies a component within the storage unit. These code numbers will also appear on labels for the master itself, additional sheets of information that relate to the master, and anywhere else that the object is referenced. Like many of the forms here, this format can be useful as a screen of a database.

Cat. #	Date	Title	DAT #	ID#	DAT Timings						Tape				Comments	CD Archive
					Begin			End			Type	TK	ips	Storage		
					h:	mm:	ss	h:	mm:	ss						
LW#1D	2/20/55	Church of the Air	1	1	0:	02:	00	0:	31:	45	1/4"	1/2	7.5	H/O	Hum throughout	RDBK
LW#2D	1/28/63	Chorus Copy-Shir L'Shabat	1	2	0:	32:	00	0:	54:	58	1/4"	1/2	7.5	H/O	Hiss, crackles throughout	RDBK
LW#3D	2/24/63	Message of Israel-Shir L'Shabot	1	3	0:	55:	20	1:	19:	25	1/4"	1/2	7.5	H/O	Distortion, dropouts @ 59:25, clicks throughout, broken splice @ 1:05:52 (ID #4 - no loss of program)	RDBK
LW#4D	2/21/65	Message of Israel-Shir L'Shabot	1	5	1:	19:	37	1:	43:	35	1/4"	1/2	7.5	H/O	Tape is badly warped, plays okay, warbling throughout	RDBK
LW#5D	12/4/66	Message of Israel-Chanukah Blessings	2	1	0:	02:	00	0:	27:	05	1/4"	1/2	7.5	H/O	Emulsion in rough shape at beginning, plays ok, distortion throughout	RDBK
LW#6D	* 5/1/67	The Last Judgement									1/4"	1/2	3.75		One channel only, slight distortion throughout	RDBK
LW#7D	5/17/67		2	2	0:	27:	11	1:	07:	55	1/4"	1/2	7.5	H/O		RDBK
LW#8D	8/10/67	Message of Israel (Yehudi Wyner)	2	3	1:	08:	05	1:	33:	55	1/4"	1/2	7.5	H/O	Tape is warped and very fragile, small dropouts throughout, hum and hiss throughout, program is rather quiet, some pops at end	RDBK
LW#9D	* 10/1/67	Bonche, Father and Son									1/4"	1/2	3.75		Tape extremely brittle, multiple breaks, dropouts, old splices stick, 1/2 track mono both sides	CD 24
LW#10D	* N/A	On the Wings of Song									1/4"	1/2	7.5	H/O	Crackles and hiss	CD 24 & RDBK
LW#11D	* 1970	Bonche-Washington									1/4"	1/4	3.75	H/O	Hissy, small dropouts	RDBK
LW#12D	* 4/10/70	Radio Interview on WGMS									1/4"	1/2	3.75	H/O	Hiss, static, two sided 1/2 track mono	RDBK
LW#13D	5/17/70	Message of Israel (A Tribute to Lazar Weiner)	2	4	1:	34:	06	2:	00:	15	1/4"	1/2	7.5	H/O	Program is rather quiet	RDBK
LW#14D	4/7/78	Lazar Weiner's 80th Anniversary Concert	3	1	0:	02:	00	0:	27:	42	1/4"	1/2	7.5	H/O	Slight dropouts and distortion, random room noises and bumps throughout; broken tape @ 27:40, nothing follows after break, track listing accompanies the tape	RDBK
LW#15D	* 5/25/72	Complete Piano Music of Yehudi Wyner & Lazar Weiner									1/4"	1/2	3.75		Light hiss, distortion, left channel dropouts	RDBK
LW#16D (side 1)	5/25/72	Complete Piano Music of Yehudi Wyner & Lazar Weiner	4	5	1:	22:	20	2:	04:	20	1/4"	1/4	7.5	H/O	Recorded on both directions, some distortion some warbling throughout	RDBK
LW#16D (side 2)	5/25/72	Complete Piano Music of Yehudi Wyner & Lazar Weiner	5	1	0:	02:	00	0:	43:	35	1/4"	1/4	7.5	H/O	brief 'static' noise @ 6:22 on source	RDBK
LW#17D	4/1/74	Yehudi Wyner-Friday Eve Service Part I	3	2	0:	27:	45	0:	55:	46	1/4"	1/2	7.5	H/O	Pops throughout, low freq. Distortion @ 29:13, low freq, hum throughout, some distortion, tape runs out at end of program	RDBK on disc with 18D
LW#18D	4/1/74	Yehudi Wyner-Friday Eve Service Part II	3	3	0:	55:	50	1:	13:	03	1/4"	1/2	7.5	H/O	Low freq. hum, some pops and dropouts throughout	RDBK on disc with 17D
LW#19D	12/6/74	A Salute to Lazar Weiner I	3	4	1:	13:	06	1:	51:	23	1/4"	1/2	7.5	H/O	Some distortion, one channel only, most of program is very quiet, many leadered off selections at the beginning of tape, some long dropouts	RDBK on disc with 20D
LW#20D	12/6/74	A Salute to Lazar Weiner II	4	1	0:	02:	00	0:	28:	25	1/4"	1/2	7.5	H/O	One channel only, some dropouts, program is rather quiet, many leadered off selections, some distortion on loud sections, outline of program included with tape	RDBK on disc with 19D
LW#21D	N/A	Folksbeine-Master I (1-7)	4	2	0:	28:	28	0:	44:	50	1/4"	1/2	15	H/O	One channel only, many leadered selections, some distortion, oxide is loose (bake before using again)	RDBK on disc with 22D

FIG. 13. Artist Archive Index for Composer/Conductor Lazar Weiner.
Courtesy of Jonathan Wyner.

14. SONG DATA SHEET

A *song data sheet* organizes the information associated with an individual track (song, composition, piece, etc.). It is sometimes formatted as part of the audio archive reel sheet (see figure 15), breaking down the project component by component (in a long, horizontal chart). This information can be used for informing album credits and for embedding into each digital file as metadata.

Track Name:		
Artist:		Release Year:
Album Name:		Track Number:
ISRC Code:	UPC Code:	Archive ID:
Genre:	Beats Per Minute:	
Bit Depth:	Sample Rate:	Output Format:
Performers:		
Composer/Songwriter:	Lyricist:	Producer:
Tracking Engineer:		
Mixing Engineer:		
Mastering Engineer:		

FIG. 14. Song Data Sheet

15. PROJECT ASSETS SUMMARY

The *project assets summary* is an index into the different media assets involved in a recording project. They are particularly useful as a form within databases for tracking all projects at a mastering house or record label. The *Archive ID* is an internal reference code used by the archivist to uniquely identify each reel, hard drive, or other asset, which is cross-referenced and further described in the archive reel sheet (see figure 15).

Artist Name:	Archive Date:	Job Number:
Project Name:		Duration:
Distribution Format:		Replicator:

	Multitrack	**Mix**	**Master**
Archive ID			
Media Type			
Sample Rate			
Bit Depth			
Studio			
Engineer			

FIG. 15. Project Assets Summary

16. AUDIO ARCHIVE REEL SHEET

Archive reel sheets reveal what's in a single audio session archive object (tape, disc, hard drive, etc., any of which can replace "reel" in your form title). While the reel sheet might be used as a label affixed to the specific tape reel or drive (see "Media Label," form 17), it can be a little big and detailed for that, and is instead commonly a file or piece of paper enclosed inside, or a view of a database. One goal of this form is to help identify the tools required to access the archive before an archeology-minded engineer actually pulls the archive from the box/shelf/drive and sticks it into a machine.

Common abbreviations:

M: Master (sometimes called a "premaster"); the version used for replicating the final recording.

S: Safety. Note that sometimes, safety copies are mono recordings made as copies of the master.

A or Alt: Alternate mixes/takes. Not used for the ultimate release copy, but good enough to be considered and not thrown away. (This can be gold, in an archive of a famous recording.)

H: Hold. Not selected for immediate use, but someone thought there was something interesting in it—like an alternate solo, or an extended arrangement, or a tune that was dropped from the final set—and decided to keep it, just in case. Also a potential source of gold.

Archive Reel Sheet

Archive ID: _____

❏ Master   ❏ Backup   ❏ Extra Material   ❏ Alternate Mix

Artist Name: Recording Date: Catalog No.:

Project Name: Duration:

Record Label: Producer: Target Format:

Bit Depth:	Tracks:	Storage Media:
❏ 16 Bit	❏ Stereo	❏ 1/4-inch Half Track
❏ 24 Bit	❏ Mono	❏ 1/4-inch Quarter Track
❏ 32 Bit	❏ Multitrack	❏ 1/2-inch Half Track
		❏ 2-inch
Sample Rate:	Record Deck/Software:	❏ Hard Drive
❏ 44.1 kHz ❏ 48 kHz		❏ DAT
❏ 88.2 kHz ❏ 96 kHz		❏ Disc
		❏ Other:
		Number _____ of _____

Tracking Engineer: _____

Mixing Engineer: _____

Mastering Engineer: _____

Replicator: _____

NOTES:

FIG. 16. Archive Reel Sheet

17. MASTER ARCHIVE CUE SHEET

A *master archive cue sheet* is a type of media label/reel sheet used by a mastering engineer to indicate what's on a master archive, this time breaking down what's on the archive song by song/cue by cue. In addition to the audio, these archives include metadata about each piece. The sheet shown in figure 16 is for a video-tape archive, as the media type.

Common terms and abbreviations:

Source Media:	Format that the project arrived on—e.g., this mix arrived at the mastering studio on a DAT.
Archive Media:	Format of the archive media. The master stored in this box is on a 3M Aud-60 videotape.
SMPTE Time Code:	The track where the SMPTE time code is written (hours, minutes, seconds, frames).
PQ Subcodes:	The track where session metadata is stored.
Actual/Access:	Locations within tracks for metadata.
Individual:	Cue duration.
Begin/End:	Time where the cue starts or stops.

Master Archive Cue Sheet

Title: "Atom Again"
Artist: Another Johnny
Company: Meetinghouse Productions
Catalog No.: AJ-2013-1

Source Media: analog/DAT
Sample Rate: 44.1 kHz
Archive Media: 3M Aud-60 Videotape
SMPTE Timecode: Audio Ch. 2
PQ Subcodes: Audio Ch. 1 @ 00:15
Timecode Begins: 00:00:00:00
Timecode End: 00:27:28:27

| Track # | Title | Begin End | SMPTE | | | | | | | | | | | |
| | | | Actual | | | | Access | | | | Individual | | | |
			Hr	Min	Sec	Fr	Hr	Min	Sec	Fr	Hr	Min	Sec	Fr
1	Baby Bat Blues	B		02	00	00		01	59	25		03	13	12
		E												
2	Notebooks	B		05	13	12		05	13	07		03	13	00
		E												
3	Missing Mattresses	B		08	26	12		08	26	07		03	39	27
		E		12	06	09		12	07	09				
4	Water Torture	B		12	25	16		12	25	11		03	21	09
		E		15	46	25		15	47	25				
5	Oh, Dahlia	B		15	49	05		15	49	00		03	05	22
		E												
6	Crab Dance	B		18	54	27		18	54	22		04	51	22
		E		23	46	19		23	47	19				
7	The Surrender of Rex Neptune	B		23	50	00		23	49	25		03	37	27
		E		27	27	27		27	28	27				
		B												
		E												
		B												
		E												
		B												
		E												
		B												
		E												
		B												
		E												

FIG. 17. Master Archive Cue Sheet

18. TAKE SHEET

A *take sheet* identifies and describes the recorded passes during a recording. In the days of audiotape, take sheets were indispensable—the way to see what was on a tape without actually listening to it. In digital systems, they remain helpful, though it is possible to do a lot of the documentation "in the box" (within the software). However, some engineers still maintain charts like this in order to document what's on a given take. For nostalgia's sake, this take sheet includes a "reel" column, which is used to reference which tape reel we're documenting. That could alternatively reference a hard drive, or just be left out. For Start and End, indicate the SMPTE stamp (or round to seconds). In a DAW, time stamps can be left out for complete takes, but can be helpful when referencing part of a take that might get comped into a track. Only one take should be marked "selected" (circled).

Some common symbols used in take sheets:

C or CT: Complete take (they made it from beginning to end).

IC or IT: Incomplete take; only part of the song is recorded.

◯   Selected take; it's been decided that you'll use it.

FS: False Start; they began the tune, but it immediately fell apart. Then they started again, playing through, without setting up a new take.

X: All Bad; unusable.

H: Hold. This can mean a variety of things: keep this track and don't change it, as we might want it for later; don't bounce this because quality is essential (usually for lead vocals); or reserve this empty track for later use.

Take Sheet

Date: January 21, 2013   **Page:**   _____ of _____

Client: J. Adams   **Phone:**   123-456-7890

Artist: Another Johnny   **Project:**   "Atom Again"

Engineer: Bruce Stevenson   **Console:**   Mackie

Format: DP   **Sample Rate:** _____ kHz **Bit Depth:** ❏ 16 ❏ 24

Reel	Take	Description	Start	End	Comments
1	1	Missing Mattresses	01:03	4:43	C
1	(2)	"	5:01	8:41	Best. Overdub guitar solo if there's time.
1	⨯1	Baby Bat Blues	8:51	8:60	FS
1	(2)	"	9:01	12:14	Best
1	3	"	12:21	15:13	H/CT. A little fast.
...					

FIG. 18. Take Sheet

19. LYRIC TAKE SHEET

A *lyric take sheet* (or just "lyric sheet") helps you identify the best performance of each line, so that the engineer can *comp together* (create a composite track from) the best ones into a single ideal track. The lyric sheet is a chart of the lyrics, phrase by phrase, with columns indicating each performance. Common symbols used are + (good) and – (bad), with a circle around the take selected for use. Song sections are indicated by indentation level, rather than text labels for "verse," "chorus," "bridge," etc.

When comping together tracks, it's easiest for the engineer to keep phrases intact, when possible, rather than replacing individual words, so the lyrics are divided into phrases on this form to support that.

In the header row, a circled take number indicates the best one. An X through it means that there was nothing usable in it. In this lyric sheet, there were two complete takes, and take 2 was better than take 1. Take 3 was a botch job. Takes 4 and 5 were partial takes, just going over some of the rough areas in hopes of getting a better performance. Note that there was a running start before the needed takes, so that the vocalist could start singing before each critical spot was cued up.

"You and Only You" 10/4/2013	1	②	~~3~~	4	5
1. What made you shave your head in Amsterdam?	−	+	−	(+)	
When you turned off the moon And walked out of the room?	+	+	−	(+)	
Did you find the crooked smile that you'd been waiting for?	+	+	−	(+)	
The skeleton key to your world away from me?	+	−		(+)	
For a while I would wonder if I broke it	+	(+)		−	
Now I know that I couldn't if I tried	+	(+)			−
I don't have your special knack for self-destruction	−	−			(+)
That's your gift and it's why I say	−	+			(+)
You and only you could make Paris a dry town	+	(+)			
Without the faintest hint of romance in the air	+	(+)			
You and only you could dissipate its sweet perfume	+	(+)			
You and only you wouldn't care	+	(+)			
2. Life's been up and down these twenty-seven years	−	(+)			
Since you left me in Spain, Running off with what's her name	−	(+)			−
Not much has come together since the day we fell apart	(+)	−			−
But for all we've been though, Yeah, I guess I'm glad to see you, still	−	(+)			
For a while I would wonder if I broke it	+	(+)			
Now I know that I couldn't if I tried	+	(+)			
I don't have your special knack for self-destruction	+	(+)			−
That's your gift and it's why I say	+	(+)			+
You and only you could make Paris a dry town	−	+			(+)
Without the faintest hint of romance in the air	−	+			(+)
You and only you could dissipate her sweet perfume	+	−			(+)
You and only you wouldn't care	+	+			(+)
You and only you wouldn't care	+	(+)			+
You and only you wouldn't care	+	(+)			−

FIG. 19. Lyric Sheet. Courtesy of Fantasy Monologue.

20. CD MASTER CHECKLIST

This *CD master checklist* is a quality control device we use at Berklee Press. Most of our products include audio recordings, and this checklist evolved over the years to help us confirm that all is well before the master goes to replication. As you can see, it includes considerations that the mastering engineer should catch (such as pops and skips) and also information that relates to our books, which they'd be likely to miss. Whatever product you create, a checklist like this can help you confirm that certain common errors or flaws are contained. We maintain similar checklists for many other dimensions of our work. If you want to buckle down on recurring problems, you can instruct whoever uses the checklist to actually check each box and then sign the sheet. That makes people more careful.

CD Master Checklist

Audio:

❑ 79:48 maximum minutes:seconds

❑ 99 tracks maximum

❑ 1 to 4 seconds between tracks

❑ Files are WAV or AIFF and *not* MP3

❑ Plays in audio-only CD player (don't test it only on a computer)

❑ CD label has project name and date of CD, content indication (audio, data, CD-plus, etc.), and whether it is intended as the actual master or a draft

Content:

❑ Performances match notation in book manuscript

❑ Examples are repeated in accordance with book's notation

❑ Tracks are in the correct order, matching "CD Tracks" page in the book

❑ Track names are correctly spelled, and rendered just like "CD Tracks" page

❑ Track numbers match "CD Tracks" page and icons in the book

❑ Countoffs/clicks are used consistently

❑ No distortion, pops, random talking, or other extraneous noise

❑ No long spaces of silence at beginning or end of tracks (more than 4 seconds)

❑ Volume levels are loud enough and consistent from track to track

❑ Information is present in both channels throughout the recording

---

FIG. 20. CD Master Checklist

21. MEDIA LABEL

A *media label* is the sticker used on a CD, audiotape, videotape, DAT, floppy disk, hard drive, or other form of media. While some of the information on the reel label or cue sheet could be included here, it is also common to keep these labels concise and then reference the other pages via catalog numbers. Figure 17 is a concise form of label, with just the most essential info. The *archive date* is important because it can help reveal which is the most up-to-date archive of a project, if there are multiple likely candidates. The Catalog Number serves as a cross-reference to additional information, whether in a database or an accompanying sheet. The example catalog number here is derived from the artist name, the year, and a sequential number for that year. This project is the studio's first one in 2013 by the artist Another Johnny.

Project Title:	"Atom Again"	Catalog Number:	AJ-2013-1
Artist:	Another Johnny	Archive Date:	November 10, 2013
Archive Description:	Master		

FIG. 21. Media Label

PART III

On the Silver Screen

These forms relate to the worlds of film and television music, where hundreds of people might be involved in a project: performers, composers, orchestrators, arrangers, directors, producers, copyright administrators, and so on. Many are non-musicians, and the forms help bridge the communication gaps between them.

Common terms and abbreviations:

S: Source cue (such as a song playing on a radio)

SFX: Sound Effects

DX: Dialogue

FX: Foley (acted out sound effects)

MX: Music

Temp: Temporary track. This is "placeholder music" used to show the type of cue desired, with the understanding that it will be replaced with original music. Here, they used three soundtracks from other films as temp tracks, abbreviated on the following few forms: "*TRY*" for the soundtrack to *Troy*, "*DVC*" for *The DaVinci Code*, and "*MI3*" for *Mission Impossible 3*.

The examples in this section are all drawn from *The Repatriation of Henry Chin* (Courtesy of Isaac Ho).

22. SPOTTING SHEET/NOTES

A *spotting sheet* lists "spotting notes," indicating where music cues are needed in a film or television soundtrack. Generally, the music editor, composer, director, and other key participants go through a cut of the picture together and identify places where music is needed and discuss what it should sound like. There are many variations of this form, with variances regarding what additional information will be included. Most essential are the cue number, start time, and description of what music is needed. They may be entered into a database, rather than existing only on paper, as the information can then be easily sorted and adapted for other purposes.

In film, cues are traditionally numbered in a form such as "1M1," which refers to the reel number (or hard drive number, but we'll use "reel" for convenience), M for music, and a sequential number within the reel. So, 4M3 is the third music cue on reel number 4. For a television show, the first number might be an episode, rather than a reel. And some films might use act or scene numbers, rather than reel numbers, particularly when they are shot digitally.

Figure 22.1 is a common horizontal form, giving more space to the notes and comments, and isolating the temp track in its own field.

SCENE 22

22M1	**In:** 00:13:07;03	**Out:** 00:15:55;10	**Duration:** 00:02:42;07
CUE: MILITARY MARCH (with somber horns)			
DESCRIPTION: The first view of the Rose Bowl surrounded by armed soldiers. Reaction shots of Henry and Elizabeth.			
TEMP: *TRY*, 02 "Troy" from 0:30			
NOTES: Duck under dialogue until:			

SCENE 23

23M1	**In:** 00:15:55;10	**Out:** 00:17:01;14	**Duration:** 00:01:06;04
CUE: SUSPENSEFUL CHASE MUSIC			
DESCRIPTION: A CLERK inspects Elizabeth's luggage. CLERK: You can't take all three suitcases.			
TEMP: *MI3*, 04 "Helluvacopter Chase" from 0:48			
NOTES: A burst of ORANGE, BLUE, and GREEN FLAMES shoot up from the trashcan. Henry kicks over the trashcan and grabs Elizabeth.			

FIG. 22.1. Spotting Notes: Horizontal Format

Here are the cues in a single table, which facilitates fitting more cues on a page, though usually with less information about each cue. The format of spotting notes will vary.

Cue	Start	Length	Video Description	Audio Description
21M1	00:12:35;16	00:00:31;53	The shuttle bus slowly snakes down a cordoned-off street lined with protesters.	SFX: The rumble of the bus's engine transitions into the low, steady drumbeat of: **MUSIC CUE: MILITARY MARCH** (Temp: *TRY*, 06 "The Greek Army and Its Defeat" from 0:00)
22M1	00:13:07;03	00:02:42;07	The first view of the Rose Bowl surrounded by armed soldiers. Reaction shots of Henry and Elizabeth.	**MUSIC CUE: Add somber horn section to MILITARY MARCH.** (Temp: *TRY*, 02 "Troy" from 0:30) MUSIC CUE: Duck under dialogue until:
23M1			A CLERK inspects Elizabeth's luggage.	CLERK: You can't take all three suitcases.
23M2	00:15:55;10	00:01:06;04	A burst of ORANGE, BLUE and GREEN FLAMES shoot up from the trashcan. Henry kicks over the trashcan and grabs Elizabeth.	HENRY: Follow me! MUSIC CUE: Begin **SUSPENSEFUL CHASE MUSIC.** (Temp: *MI3*, 04 "Helluvacopter Chase" from 0:48)
24M1			Henry and Elizabeth race toward the fence, evading soldiers.	**MUSIC CUE: SUSPENSEFUL CHASE** (continues)
24M2	00:17:01;14	00:00:19;05	Henry and Elizabeth's path is blocked by a chain link fence.	**MUSIC CUE: CHASE MUSIC TRAPPED TONE.** (Temp: *DVC*, 02 "L'esprit Des Gabriel" from 1:00) ELIZABETH: Now what? SFX: Henry lets out THREE QUICK WHISTLES.
24M3	00:17:20;19	00:00:32;00	Clyde appears and snips the chain link fence with bolt cutters.	**MUSIC CUE: SUSPENSEFUL CHASE** (resumes)
24M4			Clyde leads the way for Henry and Elizabeth to a waiting cargo van. Armed guards search nearby.	**MUSIC CUE: SUSPENSEFUL CHASE** (continues)

FIG. 22.2. Spotting Note: Single Table

23. TIMING NOTES

Once the spotting sheet exists, a number of other useful forms can be created based on it. One is the *timing notes*, which lists and sequences every single audio cue in the film, to the minutest detail. These are generated by music editors and are used to synchronize and coordinate all the project's audio cues. Another important form derived from spotting notes is the *music cue sheet* (see figure 25). "Begin" here refers to where the temp track starts.

Cue	Time	Title/Description
21M1	00:12;00	SFX: Bus engine rumbling
21M1	00:31;17	MUSIC: Temp: *TRY* "The Greek Army and Its Defeat" BEGIN 01:45;00 CROSSFADE TO:
22M1	00:43;00	MUSIC: Temp: *TRY* "Troy," BEGIN 00:30;00. NOTE: Duck under when dialogue begins. Hard out at CLERK: "You can't take all three suitcases."
23M2	01:06;04	MUSIC: Temp: *MI3* "Helluvacopter Chase," BEGIN: 00:48;00
24M2	00:19;05	MUSIC: Temp: *DVC* "L'esprit Des Gabriel." BEGIN: 01:00;00
24M3	00:28;12	MUSIC: Temp: *MI3* "Helluvacopter Chase." BEGIN 02:17;00.
...		

FIG. 23. Timing Notes

24. MASTER CUE SHEET/ INSTRUMENTATION BREAKDOWN

The *master cue sheet/instrumentation breakdown* is another descendant of the spotting notes. It is a concise listing of each musical element, with indications regarding required instrumentation. It can then be used to calculate costs and scheduling considerations for the required recording session. This example is for a film scored by a rhythm section and string orchestra, but it typically includes a complete orchestra. The numbers in the columns indicate how many of each instrumentalist is needed.

The Repatriation of Henry Chin			Strings				Rhythm				Soprano
Cue	Start	Title/Temp	Vln.	Vla.	Cl.	Bs.	Gtr.	E.Bs.	Pno.	Dr.	
21M1	00:12:35;16	Army in the Woods (Temp: *TRY* "The Greek Army and its Defeat")	4	2	4	2				6	
22M2	00:13:07;03	Elegy for Freedom (Temp: *TRY* "Troy")	4	2	4	2				6	
23M2	00:15:55;10	Follow Me! (Temp: *MI3* "Helluvacopter Chase")	4	2	4	2	1	1	1	8	
24M2	00:17:01;14	Trapped! (Temp: *DVC* "L'esprit Des Gabriel"). NOTE: a cappella vocal.									1
23M3	00:17:20;19	Cutting the Chains (Temp: *MI3* "Helluvacopter Chase")	4	2	4	2	1	1	1	8	

FIG. 24. Master Cue Sheet

25. MUSIC CUE SHEET

A *music cue sheet* lists all the music used in an audio/visual piece: a film, television show, commercial, and so on. (For the type of cue sheets used by stage managers, see form 3.) It is prepared by someone in a production company's music department, such as a music editor at a film studio. This form is another descendent of the spotting notes.

Music cue sheets are circulated to everyone with a stake in the music's ownership, before ultimately being provided to the appropriate performance rights agencies (PROs), who then disburse performance royalties to the copyright owners. Production rights agencies offer templates for cue sheets on their websites; the required information is essentially the same between them. It is sometimes possible to submit these to the PROs online, rather than use the paper form, but compiling the information in a sharable/paper form is helpful for communication, verification, and documentation purposes.

There are two types of information on a cue sheet: info about the main work where the music is used, and info about the music's legal status—specifically, who owns the copyright (writers, lyricists, and publishers).

Figure 25 shows a few lines from a cue sheet for a television program. Notice that the song "Debrief" has two songwriters who split the writers' share 50/50.

Common Abbreviations:
- BI: Background Instrumental
- BV: Background Vocal
- ET: End Title (Closing/Credits)
- L: Logo
- MT: Main Title (Opening)
- P: Publisher
- T: Theme
- VI: Visual Instrumental
- VV: Visual Vocal
- W: Writer

Music Cue Sheet

PRODUCTION INFORMATION

Media Title:	*The Repatriation of Henry Chin*	**Type:**	Television Series
Episode Title:	"Up on the Hill"	**Episode Number:**	Season 1, Number 9
Broadcast Date:	January 9, 2015	**Program Length:**	44 minutes
Production Company/Contact:		**Network:**	WXYZ-TV

Repatriation Production Company, LLC
100 Betty's Way
Los Angeles, CA 90012
Attn: Judy Liu
123-456-7890

CUE INFORMATION

Cue #	Title	Usage	Duration	Copyright Distribution		PRO
1M1	Henry	L	5	W:	Clyde Wilson	BMI
				P:	Clyde Wilson Productions	BMI
1M2	"Repatriation" Main Theme	MT	0:31	W:	Elizabeth Chin	ASCAP
				P:	Elizabeth Chin Publishing Co.	ASCAP
1M3	Mountains Underscore	BI	0:45	W:	Don Morgan	ASCAP
				P:	Don Morgan Publishing Co.	ASCAP
1M6	Debrief	VV	3:23	W:	Don Morgan	ASCAP
				W:	Clyde Wilson	BMI
				P:	Don Morgan Publishing Co.	SESAC
...						

FIG. 25. Music Cue Sheet

PART IV

On the Road

Musicians on tour have to track and negotiate issues related to travel, as well as conduct their business outside of an organized office environment. These details will generally be prepared in advance of a tour, and sometimes updated during it. Travel is often a complex undertaking, and forms like the ones in this section can greatly reduce risk of on-the-road mishaps. These forms are often created and maintained by a band manager.

26. ASSETS INVENTORY

An *assets inventory* is a detailed checklist that is particularly useful on tour, but also for recording studios, concert halls, and music organizations generally that stock a lot of gear. It lists all physical assets for insurance purposes, as well as serving as a checklist of items to bring on tour or have on hand. Databases with all this information can be the best way to maintain this information, as it can become quite extensive, particularly for school music programs, orchestras, music stores, and others. Photos of each item can help identify and recover them in the case of theft.

Asset Name	Description	Brand/Maker/ Model	Year Made	Serial Number, Identifying Marks	Insured Value	Owner/ User
Laptop	MacBook Pro	Apple	2005	C02IN3YFLZ7N	$2,500	Eugenia
Bass Guitar	4-string bubinga wood electric bass	Warwick Corvette Pro	2001	6-077812-00; "J" engraved into body	$800	Ethan
Clarinet	B♭ wood clarinet	Vijon	1950?	B-3937	$400	Sam
¼ Inch Cables	5@20', 10@6'	Monster	2008	Red tape on 20' plugs, green tape on 6' plugs	$15 each	Betsy
…						

FIG. 26. Assets Inventory

27. TOUR ITINERARY

A *tour itinerary* summarizes all the information tour participants need to know for their tour: where to be, when to be there, how to prepare, what to expect. Sending this information via email keeps it accessible from everyone's smartphone.

Travel Info			
Flight to/from Nashville		**Depart**	**Arrive**
Go There: Thursday, 10/17 Southwest 3481		BOS 9:05 A.M.	BNA 10:50 A.M.
Come Home: Monday, 10/22 Southwest 262		BNA 10:50 A.M.	BOS 2:20 P.M.
Private Bus to/from Memphis			
Go There: Sunday, 10/20	7:00 A.M. Departure from Brentwood Suites Lobby		
Return: Sunday, 10/20	11:30 P.M.		

Hotel	Concert/Rehearsal Venues	
Brentwood Suites	Grand Ole Opry	New Daisy Theatre
622 Church Street	2804 Opryland Drive	330 Beal Street
East Brentwood, TN 37027	Nashville, TN 37214	Memphis, TN 38013
1-866-277-4009	1-800-733-6779	(901) 525-8979

Itinerary

Date	Name/Type	Location	Start	End	Notes
10/17	Flight	BOS to BNA	9:05 A.M.	10:50 A.M.	Arrive an hour early. Tickets/timing/gate info will come via email and text. Our bus will bring us from the airport to the hotel. No other events planned, optional dinner at the hotel at 6:00 P.M.
10/18	Breakfast	Hotel	8:30 A.M.	9:30 A.M.	Optional
	Dress Rehearsal	Grand Ole Opry	10:00 A.M.	Noon	Bus leaves hotel at 9:40. **Let me know if you have other arrangements.**
	Concert	Grand Ole Opry	6:30 P.M.	10:30 P.M.	Bus leaves hotel at 6:10. Be ready for pictures at 6:45.
10/19	Dinner	Monell's 1235 6th Avenue North	5:00 P.M.	6:30 P.M.	Optional, but potentially life-changing. Bus leaves from hotel at 4:30.
	Concert	Grand Ole Opry	7:30 P.M.	10:30 P.M.	Bus leaves hotel at 6:10.
10/20	To Memphis	Bus leaves from hotel	7:00 A.M.	11:30 P.M.	We're all hanging together all day for everything. Meals provided on bus.
	Concert	New Daisy	2:00 P.M.	6:00 P.M.	
...					

Emergency Contact

Eugenia at 123-456-7890 (ejs1969@hotmail.com). If you're going to be late, have an emergency, or have any questions, call/text me.

FIG. 27. Tour Itinerary

28. TOUR CHECKLIST

Loading gear into cars is an obnoxious dimension of the musician's lifestyle. But it is even more obnoxious to arrive at a gig having forgotten something important. Sure, you're likely to remember your guitar, but if you forget to bring a cable, your guitar becomes useless. And what about backup batteries for your effects pedals? What about the W-9 form? What about your EpiPen? Checklists can help you remember the stupid stuff. You might have a page or two for each band member, and each dimension of stuff you want to remember. This sample gives a format for a checklist and some ideas for what dimensions of items you might want to track.

Guitar-Related Gear			
	Fender	Break in new strings on all guitars	
	Gibson	Change batteries in all guitars and pedals	
	Banjo	Uke	
	2 sets of extra strings for each instrument	Repair kit	
	Tuner	Music stand	
	Backup strap	2 extra picks	
	Pedal board	10 backup 9-volt batteries	
	Marshall amp	Fender amp	
	Practice amp	3 guitar stands	
Wardrobe/Personal			
	4 concert shirts	4 concert pants	
	2 bath towels	Makeup kit	
	EpiPen	Camera	
	fingernail kit		
Audio			
	6 dynamic mics	4 vocal mics	
	6 12-foot XLR cables	Snake	
	6 6-foot quarter-inch cables	4 20-foot quarter-inch cables	
	mic stands	Compressor	
	4 pop filters	Reverb	
	2 DI boxes	Metronome	
	Mixing console	Extra tubes	
	4 Monitors	4 headphones	
	Blank CDRs	Alesis HD recorder	
	Splitter	Cable repair kit	
	Sharpie	Masking tape	

Merch		
	T-shirts	CDs	
	Credit card reader	Cash box	
	Cash for change	Flyers	
Vehicle/Travel		
	Van	2 weeks before, check oil, tires (including spare), etc.	
	Battery charger	Cell phone charger cables	
	Spare tire	Air compressor	
	AAA card (confirm it's not expired)	Confirm emissions inspection sticker, registration, and drivers' licenses are not expired	
	Snacks, Water	Trash bags	
	GPS	Directions to venues	
	Road atlas	Extra key to van	
	Flashlight	Cooler	
	Coffee maker	Coffee	
	Bottle opener/Corkscrew	Kitchen knife	
Documents/Business		
	W-9 form	Passports	
	Business cards	Travel receipts bag	
	Confirm insurance is up to date	Copy of *Project Management for Musicians*	
	Copies of contracts	3 copies of press kit	
	Photo release forms (blank)	Emergency contact list, and other forms in this book	
Other		
	Batteries: AA, AAA, 9V	Gaffers tape	
	Quarters for laundry/parking meters	Hot sauce	
	First aid kit	Dog leash	
	…		

FIG. 28. Tour Checklist

29. TRAVEL INSTRUCTIONS

Circulating travel tips/directions to everyone traveling under your charge can reduce confusion, catastrophes, and risk. Particularly with complex situations, such as transporting a children's orchestra internationally, such lists can be invaluable—like this set based on one from *From the Top*, an organization that frequently transports first-time world travelers. Of course, you should customize the advice to each trip's specific circumstances.

Travel Instructions

Before Booking Your Flight

1. Confirm with your airline that your instrument meets the size requirements for the aircraft. Determine whether you need to buy a seat for your instrument. If you do, you might need to arrange for a seat belt extension.

2. Confirm that your driver's license, passport, or other travel documents are current and won't expire during the trip.

3. If you have any rented or borrowed gear, confirm with their owner that you are allowed to travel with it.

4. Confirm that your gear is insured for this trip.

5. Arrange for transportation to and from the airports, and consider whether your instrument will fit in a standard taxi. We do NOT arrange for ground transportation.

6. If you need a wheelchair or other special assistance, arrange for one with the airport, and also let us know. Also let us know if you have any medical condition that might affect your ability to fly.

7. Get a hard case with wheels for your instrument, if possible.

8. Make two checklists: one of everything you need to bring, and one listing all your luggage items.

24 Hours Before Flight

1. Check your flight's status. Let us know if you will be delayed by more than an hour.

2. Print your boarding pass at home, and prepay for any luggage.

3. Reconfirm your ground transportation to and from the airport.

4. Confirm that any instrument-related supplies that might alert the TSA are either packed with gels/liquids (such as trombone slide grease), packed in your bags (such as oboe reed knives), or left at home (pyrotechnics).

5. Prepare your instrument for flight travel. Loosen your strings and bow, and make sure any potentially loose parts are secure.

6. Make sure your bags look distinctive. For example, you could tie a bright ribbon on each handle.

Travel Day

1. Confirm your flight status before you leave your house.

2. Arrive at the airport two hours before your flight.

3. If you have any problems, any questions, or are significantly delayed, call Bo. [Contact info prominently included.]

FIG. 29. Travel Instructions

30. EMERGENCY CONTACT LIST/ MEDICAL INFO SHEET

Whoever is in charge of the tour (band manager and/or leader) should keep a list of emergency contact information for everyone involved. There might be legal considerations regarding the privacy of this information, so don't make this information public. But get what information you can.

Name of Tour Member	Emergency Contact 1 Name/Relationship/ Phone Numbers/ Address	Emergency Contact 2 Name/Relationship/ Phone Numbers/ Address	Health Concerns, Allergies, Medications

FIG. 30. Emergency Contact List/Medical Info Sheet

31. MERCHANDISE SALES REGISTER

When you sell merch at gigs, a *sales register* logs information about your merchandise sales transactions. This helps you track what kinds of merch sells well in different locations, know how much merch you have left (and if you need to order more), and inform whether you are actually selling merch or if it is walking away on its own accord. It's also important for tax purposes. Ideally, you'll have a higher tech system take care of all this, like an app, spreadsheet, or actual cash register/POS (point of sale) system. But sometimes, you need to track it manually, with pen and paper, and a form like this can facilitate your calculating and tracking the essential information. Here's a simple sales register, ready to log whatever you want to sell.

Date	Description	Total
7/9/13	T-Shirt S	21
	T-Shirt L	42
	2 T-Shirts (S, L), 1 CD (FM)	57.75
	CD (GM)	0
...		

FIG. 31.1. Simple Sales Register

You can minimize the amount of required writing by using a more detailed register. This works best if you only have a few items to sell, as it can get cumbersome otherwise, but in certain circumstances, it is the quickest way to record a transaction. In figure 31.2, the "Seller" is the person working the table. The "Comment" column is used to explain discounted sales or giveaways (which are tax write-offs), or perhaps customer questions. The "Start" row is the number of existing inventory before that day's sales began (with the total amount being the money in the cash box to be used for making change). The "Total Sales" row summarizes the transactions, and the End row is the end of night existing inventory, which can get moved to the "Start" row the next night. The form gets reconciled before selling starts the next day (physical inventory gets counted), and the person who reconciles it signs and dates the bottom. This way, you can reconcile the till and hopefully solve problems (like too many freebies to girls with cute puppies) before they get out of hand.

This register factors in taxes. (Stop sniggering.) Alternatively, you could fold taxes into the item price and deduct it later, to simplify making change. Just be sure that if the venue takes a cut of merch sales, their share is calculated on the pre-tax price.

Detailed Sales Register

Date: 7/9/13   **Venue:** Dahlia's   **City:** Cambridge, MA   **Seller:** Gene

	T-Shirts: $20				CDs: $15		Comment	Total Pre-Tax	Tax	Total
	S	M	L	XL	Fantasy Monologue	Greatest Misses			5%	
Start	50	50	50	50	50	25				$200
	1							20	1	21
			2					40	2	42
	1		1		1		Wanted kids' size	55	2.75	57.75
						1	Free to girl with cute puppy			0
Total Sales	2		3		1	1				120.75
End	48	50	47	50	49	24				320.75

Reconciled by: _____ Date: _____

FIG. 31.2. Detailed Sales Register

32. VENUE LIST

A *venue list* helps the band manager to track critical information about different gig venues.

Name/Address	Fee Structure	Seats	Booking Contact	Notes	Last Contact
Dahlia's Nyack, NY	We pay $500, set ticket price and keep 100% of proceeds	300	Bo 123-456-7890 bo@email.com	Live music Saturday nights	Voicemail 7/20
Hart Beat Hartford, CT				Recommended by CS	Must call
The Dreggs Ayer, MA	They pay us $800 and keep door	150	Su 987-654-3210 su@email.net	Book Mondays at least 60 days in advance	Email 8/30
JB's Lincolnville, ME				Recommended by SS	Must Call

FIG. 32. Venue List

33. VENUE SUMMARY SHEET

A *venue summary sheet* tracks all essential information about a venue for the artist's reference, rather than as an agreement with a venue (see "Booking Sheet," form 65). Before the gig, it serves as a checklist of information you want to gather. Afterwards, it is a reference point and summary, to jog your memory about the details and possibly inform whether you want to play there again. Take some photos of every venue you play—the performance space, the backstage areas, and the people who work there—to help you remember the details.

Venue Name: **Capacity:**   **Would We Return?**

Venue Summary:

Audience Summary:

Address:

Contact Name/Title: **Phone:**   **Email:**

Opens: _____   Closes: _____   Load-In Time: _____   Performance Time: _____

Set Length: _____   Load-In Notes: _____

FEATURES/RATINGS   **Overall:** _____

Vibe: _____   Ease: _____   Features: _____   X Factor: _____

Parking: _____   Loading Dock: _____   Green Room: _____   Secure Storage: _____

Door Person: _____   Bouncer: _____   Merch Table: _____   Stage: _____

Close Food/Coffee Options: _____

SUPPORT

Type	Contact	Quality	Costs	Description
Sound				
Lighting				
Promo				
Runner				
Stage Crew				
Merch				

FINANCIAL

Cost of Entry/Band Payment: _____   House Cut of Merch: _____

Comp Tickets Limit: _____

Date	Seats Sold	Notes

ATTACHMENTS

❑ Booking Sheet/Contract   ❑ Rider   ❑ Guest List

FIG. 33. Venue Summary Sheet

34. BOOKING REQUEST FORM

A *booking request form* (or "offer form") is generally used by artist management companies working with established acts. These forms often appear on websites. They field prospective client queries to see if the artist wants to do the gig. The prospective client fills in the information. The management company might consult with the artist and then get back to the client to negotiate an actual contract. So, this form is non-binding, intended as an initial communication in advance of a formal agreement, unlike a "Booking Sheet" (see form 65).

Artist		
Name of Requested Artist:		
Other Arists Appearing at Event:		
Event Details		
Venue Name:	Type of Event:	
Address/City/State:		
URL:		
Event Date(s):	Number of Shows:	Start Time:	End Time:
Capacity:	Do you provide sound/ engineer/lighting?	
❏ Indoors ❏ Outdoors ❏ All Ages Admitted ❏ 18+ Admitted ❏ Alcohol Served ❏ Food Served ❏ Security Provided		
Other Event Details:		
Compensation Terms		
Offer Amount/Guarantee:	Ticket Price:	Artist's Door Percentage:
Travel/Expense Allowance/Terms:	Merch Split Percentage:	
What promotional efforts you will provide:		
Contact Details		
Name:	Company:	
Phone:	Email:	Best time to call:
Note: Submitting this form does not guarantee your booking. We will contact you to discuss it further. If we come to terms, a formal contract will follow.		

FIG. 34. Booking Request Form

PART V

PR and Marketing

Musicians are increasingly doing their own promotional activities. These are some of the standard marketing forms for getting the word out about your performances, new recordings, and other newsworthy activities.

35. ONE-SHEET

A *one-sheet* is a single-page flyer sent around to raise awareness of a new product, such as an album or a concert. It is like a cross between a press release and an advertisement: more graphical than a press release, more informative than an ad—bigger than a business card, smaller than a press kit. Think of it as a quick "elevator pitch" to spark interest from a radio DJ, club booker, music writer, or other press/media contact, who will expect that it be accompanied by a recording. A stack of one-sheets can be available at trade shows or concerts.

Figure 35 is a one-sheet for the band Altered Five. Its intent is to create awareness for a new album release. Typical sections are a summary of the news to be shared, the artist's history, some talking points, a track listing, contact information, graphics of the band and latest product, and a link to the website, where more detailed information can be found

ALTERED FIVE |Gotta Earn It

Proclaimed "a staple of the Midwest's band scene" and "a festival favorite" by the *Milwaukee Journal-Sentinel*, Altered Five's delectable brew of blues and soul has a wide audience taking notice. The group's sophomore album, *Gotta Earn* It, is a 10-song set featuring seven originals. According to the *Minneapolis Star Tribune*, frontman Jeff Taylor's voice is "gloriously gritty." The *Shepherd Express* simply states he sounds like "a voice from Stax/Volt 45s."

Altered Five formed in 2002 and quickly gained a reputation for its inventive arrangements and distinctive sound. *Isthmus* magazine called the band "a rising blues unit" and *OnMilwaukee.com* declared, "The group delivers the element of surprise."

On the quintet's new release, "JT" Taylor's powerful voice anchors the sound and drives home the message in songs like the brooding ballad "Three Wishes," the wistful, burning blues of "Older, Wiser, Richer," and the yearning "Mona Lisa." The rhythm section of drummer Scott Schroedl and bassist Mark Solveson grooves hard and enjoys telepathic interaction with keyboardist Ray Tevich and guitarist Jeff Schroedl. *Guitar World* raves that Schroedl has "hi-tech chops" and contributes "superlative solo work." The group also puts its stamp on three covers: a driving, bluesified take on the early Marvin Gaye hit "Ain't That Peculiar"; a revved-up reading of Buddy Guy's 1961 Chess recording "Watch Yourself"; and the cool, sassy groove of another Motown original, "You've Got to Earn It."

It's been said that "the blues is a feeling," so when the *Minneapolis Star Tribune* states that the band is a "righteous blast," you know they play it right.

Testimonial:

"As authentic as a tangy Memphis soul stew, Altered Five breathes fire into deep groove, original R&B and blues. Led by the passion and polish of barrel-chested singer Jeff 'JT' Taylor and the explosive, fret-bending guitarist Jeff Schroedl, the five blues brothers play vital music that nurtures the spirit and moves the body." —*Dave Rubin, Award-winning blues journalist*

Selling Points:

- October 20 mailing to national blues radio; 10-week campaign
- Separate PR program to press, blogs & other media; 3+ months
- Band has done many recording sessions for Hal Leonard Pub. & opened for Walter Trout, Junior Brown, Popa Chubby & others.

Track Listing:
1. Ain't That Peculiar
2. Three Wishes
3. You've Got to Earn It
4. Keep the Best
5. Older, Wiser, Richer
6. Mona Lisa
7. Tight Spot
8. Dynamite
9. Watch Yourself
10. Bounce Back

Record Label: Conclave/Cold Wind
Digital Distribution: IODA
Physical Distribution: MVD
Radio Promo: Todd Glazer Prod.
Press/Publicity: Doug Deutsch PR

Release Date: Nov. 13, 2012
File Under: Blues
Suggested Retail: $12.99
Catalog Number: CWR112
Format: CD

Website: www.alteredfive.com
Phone: XXX-XXX-XXXX

0 41871 12101 2

FIG. 35. One-Sheet for a Record Release. Courtesy of Altered Five.

36. POSTCARD

One-sheets can also take the form of postcards. Below is a postcard used in a marketing campaign for my book *Project Management for Musicians*. It's a cheap way to get a direct connection to your intended fans. For direct mail campaigns like this, it is more effective if you tell the recipient exactly what to do and clarify how it will make their life better, rather than just shouting that something exists. In this case, we offered a free product to teachers who might use it as a textbook.

FIG. 36. Postcard for Product Release (Front and Back). The front is formatted to add a mailing address and postage.

37. PRESS RELEASE

A *press release* is a communication that informs media outlets of news that they might be interested in publishing. Sometimes, recipients will use the press release as an information point, and then will contact an artist to do an in-depth interview that will result in an original piece. Other times, the publication will simply run the press release in its original form, or to varying degrees of modification.

Press releases follow a fairly standard format. They begin with a line saying when the information can be made public. (Usually, these are marked "For immediate release" in our industry, but you might have reason to request a delay.) There is then a headline designed to grab the reader's attention. The body of the release presents all the details, generally in order of most topical to more general information. It ends with contact information regarding whom to contact for further information. Ending it with ### is an old newspaper convention that indicates the end of an article. Include it to show that you are a hard-boiled writer.

The following press release template is by Susan Lindsay, half of the Celtic duo "The Lindsays." She customizes it for each gig.

FOR IMMEDIATE RELEASE

Irish Music to Go Outside the Box at [Venue Name].

Celtic duo The Lindsays to perform at [venue name] in [address, city, state] on [day of the week and date, time].

On [day/date] from [time], the Lindsays, a Massachusetts-based husband-and-wife Celtic duo, will perform at [venue name, address, city, state, etc.]. Tickets are [insert prices]. The Lindsays have a unique sound planted firmly in the Irish tradition but blending instruments, rhythms, and textures from other styles, from blues to jazz to world. [In this concert, they will be joined by master guitarist Tom Rohde of Lusby, Maryland, and percussionist Salil Sachdev, also of Massachusetts.] For more information, visit www. irishmusic.us.

About the Lindsays
The Lindsays are a husband-and-wife Celtic duo that, for more than ten years, have created an eclectic fusion of Irish ballads, traditional jigs and reels, and contemporary rock and folk for an honest acoustic delivery—with an edge.
[Info about guest artists]
[Info about the venue]
Contact Susan Lindsay at [phone, email] for more information.
# # #

FIG. 37. Press Release Template. Courtesy of Susan Lindsay.

38. REPERTOIRE LIST

A *repertoire list* (or *song list*, or *playlist*) is a more-or-less complete itemization of music that an artist is ready to perform. This kind of list is common among GB (general business) bands and is used to help clients choose what music will be performed at an event (and perhaps, to show off an artist's capabilities). A wedding band, for instance, might have a repertoire list posted on their website as a marketing tool. This is generally for the client's benefit, rather than the performers' use. A set list is then derived from the complete repertoire list, which might be hundreds of songs long. Repertoire lists typically include the song title and the original artist most commonly associated with each song (or the version that the artist's rendition most closely resembles). Songs are often categorized by theme and sorted alphabetically by title, as clients are likely to know the song's title first and the songwriter or artist second. On a website, linking to lyrics is helpful, particularly for selections used ceremoniously. Songs like Willie Nelson's "Always on My Mind" are somehow popular first dance songs at weddings, even though the lyrics mourn the end of a relationship. The dark side of a great title....

JAZZ

"A Train" by Duke Ellington/Billy Strayhorn
"All of Me" by Simons and Marks
"Autumn Leaves" by Vernon Duke
...

SUMMERTIME SONGS

"All Summer Long" by the Beach Boys
"A Dog Is a Man's Best Friend" by Angelina
"All I Want Is You" by U2
"American Girl" by Tom Petty
...

FIRST DANCE/PARENTS' DANCE

"A Moment Like This" by Kelly Clarkson
"At Last" by Etta James
"Always on My Mind" by Willie Nelson
...

FIG. 38. Repertoire List

39. MARKETING CAMPAIGN TIMELINE

Marketing campaigns for album releases, tours, and other important events are precisely timed. Typically, a marketing campaign manager will draw up a timeline showing the milestones for the campaign. The relative timing tends to be fairly consistent between projects, so if you do multiple similar campaigns, the timeline can be somewhat reusable.

The version in figure 39.1 is a variation of a *Gantt chart*—a two-dimensional timeline with bars under a line of dates that show the durations of each task or phase of a project, such as an album release campaign. This style of chart lets you see concurrent activities. At the top is a timeline of dates and major project milestones, with the most significant one (the album launch) emphasized. Below the timeline are two sections: one showing data for the product release schedule, and the other showing when various marketing activities will hit. The product release schedule features bars indicating the duration when each element will be available. Below, the marketing schedule is organized as a series of events connected back up to the timeline—instances in time when they are due or go live, rather than as a number of continuous episodes. At the bottom of the chart, the general phases of the campaign's lifecycle are indicated, as guiding principles for future development.

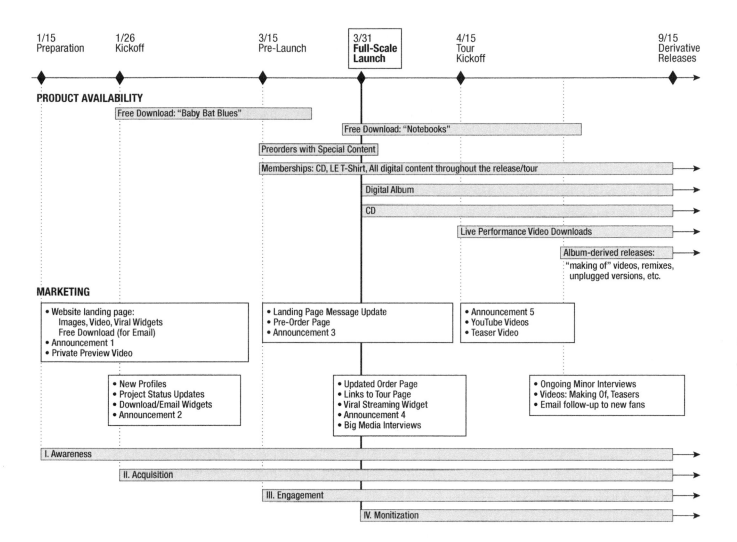

FIG. 39.1. Gantt-Style Marketing Timeline. This example was developed in collaboration with Mike King. Mike discusses the theory behind this marketing process in his excellent Berklee Online course, *Music Business Trends and Strategies* (http://online.berklee.edu).

Figure 39.2 is another style of marketing timeline. This type focuses more on tracking progress and delegating tasks (to whomever is "Responsible" for their completion).

Campaign for Album Release on March 4	Responsible	Date Due	Status
6 MONTHS OUT			
Finalize website			
Finalize marketing campaign general approach			
Assemble team, finalize agreement/contracts			
Finalize release date			
Start accumulating photos and art ideas			
Schedule venue for release event			
5 MONTHS OUT			
Write/approve copy for press release			
Write/approve copy for advance media outreach			
Develop media list			
Print 25 promo/mockup copies of CD			
Do photo shoot for marketing shots			
4 MONTHS OUT			
Pitch magazines for articles			
14 WEEKS OUT			
Send EPK link to advance readers to get quotes			
Secure interviews			
Print 1,000 copies of final CD			
Confirm artist's social media sites are current, active, and ready to receive release announcement and materials			
Email Blast 1: Announce event/ Free download of single			
10 WEEKS OUT			
Receive final CDs			
Draft/approve one-sheet			
Order printed materials, envelopes, etc. for press outreach			
Finalize EPK			
8 WEEKS OUT			
Radio promo begins (if applicable)			
Release a single			
Email Blast 2: Free Download of video teaser			
6 WEEKS OUT			
Email Blast 3: Announce fan special offer			

4 WEEKS OUT			
Choose online distribution platforms			
Announce event on relevant community calendars			
Finalize other promotional items/giveaways/door prizes			
Email Blast 4: Announce pre-sales			
2–3 WEEKS OUT			
Hang posters			
Send social media invitations			
Send press release to local press			
1 WEEK OUT			
Confirm correct info on all Internet announcements			
Determine third party retail outlets			
Email Blast 5: Event details			
DAY OF EVENT			
Do radio interview/live chat (if applicable)			
Hang signs at event			
Release third party online retail			
Email Blast 6: See you tonight			
WEEK AFTER			
Post-mortem meeting			
Confirm all invoices received/in process			
Give artist "ongoing marketing" pack			
Share reviews and photos via social media			
Email Blast 7: Thanks, and please write positive reviews			
2 WEEKS AFTER			
Release live video of concert			
Release live performance single			
Release files for remix			
Have online event via StageIt			
ONGOING			
Email, remixes, live show videos, etc.			
…			

FIG. 39.2. Task Status–Oriented Marketing Campaign Timeline

PART VI

At the Office

The forms in this section will help you gain control of your finances. They are standardized accounting documents, but customized for likely scenarios in the music industry.

40. PROFIT/LOSS FORM

A *P/L (profit/loss) form* is a financial document that shows all sources of income and expense, totaled up at the bottom to reveal the actual profit. The "Gig P/L Form" below shows that the best-paid person in this scenario is the booking agent. The gear rental agency is also doing well on this gig.

	Item	Description	Units Sold	Gross	Net	Total
Income:						
	Fee:	Total paid by venue	1 night	$1,500	$1,500	$1,500
	CDs:	$15 price – $5 production cost = $10 profit/unit	10	150	100	100
	T-Shirts:	$20 price – $5 production cost = $15 profit/unit	4	$80	$60	60
					Total Income:	1660
Expenses:						
	PA Rental:	$300				300
	Booking Fee:	15% of fee				225
	Transportation:	$.40 per mile	80	$32		32
					Total Expenses:	$557
					Total Profit:	$1,103
Payment Per Musician:		4 musicians, even split				$275.75

FIG. 40. Gig Profit/Loss Form

41. TOUR BUDGET

A *tour budget* is another view of a P/L form. This one breaks down the expense for each stop on the tour, also factoring in lump sums before the gig started.

Title	Pre Tour	3/1	3/2	3/3	3/4	3/5	3/6	3/7	Estimated Total
INCOME									
Contributions	5,000								5,000
Performance									
Fee			300	500	500	300	250		1,850
Door			100	0	200	100	100		500
Merchandise									
CDs			50	70	70	50	50		290
T-Shirts			30	50	50	30	30		190
Total Income	**5,000**	**0**	**480**	**620**	**820**	**480**	**430**	**0**	**7,830**
EXPENSES									
Travel									
Accommodations		300	300	300	300	300	300	300	2,100
Gas		40	25	25	25	25	25	40	205
Food		200	200	200	200	200	200	200	1,400
Art									
Photography (already paid)									500
Ads									250
Merchandise									
CDs	16,805								16,805
T-Shirts (includes 25% contingency over quote)	750								750
Wardrobe	?								?
Total Expenses	**17,555**	**540**	**525**	**525**	**525**	**525**	**525**	**540**	**22,010**
TOTAL	**-12,555**	**-540**	**-45**	**95**	**295**	**-45**	**-95**	**-540**	**-14,180**

FIG. 41. Tour Budget

42. BUDGET-TO-ACTUAL RECONCILIATION

A *budget-to-actual reconciliation* report tracks how well you are doing at estimating your expenses. The *budgeted* amount is what you anticipated the amount would be before any money changed hands. You can see, this budget was "balanced," which means that the income and expenses worked out to the same amount. The *actual* amount is what the final number is. By calculating the difference between your dreams and reality, you can figure out the Variance column to see how realistic your expectations were.

Below, the predicted income turned out to be conservative (bringing in 25 percent more than anticipated), and the artists kept close control over expenses as well, saving 10 percent from what they anticipated. The reduced expenses get added to the increased profit for a total of 35 percent more overall income than anticipated. This band was hoping to break even, and they turned a profit. I hope that happens to you too!

	Budget	Actual	Difference	% Variance
INCOME				
Donations	5,620	7,270	1,650	29%
Merch Sales	530	600	70	13%
Performance	1,350	1,486	136	10%
Total Income	**7,500**	**9,356**	**1,856**	**35%**
EXPENSES				
CD Production	6,000	5,400	600	10%
Merch	750	668	82	11%
Art	750	700	50	7%
Total Expenses	**7,500**	**6,768**	**+ 732**	**10%**
TOTAL	**0**	**2,588**	**2,588**	**35%**

FIG. 42. Budget-to-Actual Reconciliation

43. INVOICE

When a professional service is completed and approved, the provider should immediately give the client an *invoice*. Invoices serve two main purposes. First, they notify a client that a payment is due. Second, they provide a record of the transaction, which is useful if you get audited, among other things. You can turn an invoice into a receipt by marking it "paid."

The invoice should indicate the client's name, project name, work description, and what the payment terms of the invoice are, such as "Payable within 30 days" or "Payable upon receipt." If there are code numbers to help identify clients, projects, or transactions, those can be helpful as well. Include contact information for the client and the service provider.

Invoice

To: Berklee Press
                  Attn: Jonathan Feist, Editor in Chief
                  1140 Boylston Street
                  Boston, MA 02215

From: Raj Peal, Artist Manager

Date Submitted: March 22, 2013

Project: Songwriting for Film DVD

Artist: Zoë Munkle

Description	Amount
Guitar for recording session	$250
Parking	$12
TOTAL DUE:	**$262**

Payable upon receipt. Make check out to Zoë Munkle, and mail it to:
     Raj Peal
     123 Sarah Circle
     Boston, MA 02215

FIG. 43. Invoice

PART VII

Music Project Management

Project management is the technique of deliberately and strategically getting things done. Most industries, from automobile manufacturing to software development to the military, have their own specific systems, and the music industry benefits from careful approaches to work as much as anyone does. Roughly, you can divide project management tools into two broad categories: imagining the work and making sure it gets done. Get it right, and project management is your ticket to making dreams come true. My book *Project Management for Musicians* (Berklee Press, 2013) covers these tools and many others in greater detail.

44. DESIGN SPECIFICATION

A *design specification* (or *design spec*) is a written clarification given to a graphic designer hired to create a poster, album cover, t-shirt, or other commissioned art. It articulates the required conceptual goals and technical parameters of what is to be created. Ideally, it is preceded by a real-time conversation about the work needed. It also is generally preceded by a conversation about the artist's compensation.

Design specs are often accompanied by documents or links to completed art, either as examples of well-executed pieces to be emulated or horrific ones to be avoided. For *Project Management for Musicians*, as a starting point, we suggested to designer Jamie de Rooij that he look at a marketing piece for an ad campaign for the book's companion online course, shown in figure 44.1.a. Ultimately, he went another route (similarly, avoiding the admittedly over-wrought/complex suggestion about an old concert poster design), and came up with the design in figure 44.1.b, which worked really well. (See a color version at www.projectmanagementformusicians.com.) Jamie's design combines a variety of elements suggested in the design spec: an audio level meter, a piano keyboard, and if you track down the color version, you'll see a rainbow color scheme against the black, to combine the ideas of technology, music, and vision.

(a)   (b)

FIG. 44.1. (a) Model Art for Online Course (b) Finished Book Cover

Book Cover for *Project Management for Musicians*

SPECS: 8.5 x 11
1/8-inch bleed
1/4-inch between edge and text
Include printer guides
Deliver 300 DPI native Photoshop, Illustrator, or InDesign file, and also a reference PDF

Predetermined Layout
Standard red Berklee Press emblem in top right corner, black banner with BISAC header at top left

Cover Text

Code:	Music Business: Project Management
Title:	Project Management for Musicians
Subtitle:	Recordings, Concerts, Tours, Studios, and More
Author:	Jonathan Feist

Font Treatment
Strong, classical font, easy to read, and not too frilly. Keep "Project Management" and "for Musicians" together, if words need to be separated. Word "for" can be smaller if it's distracting.

Art Concept
Primarily text, though a graphic concept might work. Three potential ideas:

1. Base it on the graphics we did for the online course, with a flow chart. Colors worked well there, and it had a good response.

2. Generate a simple graphic, using elements from different dimensions of music, such as sound engineering (a meter?), a keyboard/guitar, or some other indication of music being made, but genre neutral.

3. Original *West-Side Story* concert poster type text, with the ladders and dancers, but here with silhouette musicians interacting with the letters.

Book Description
Creative, comprehensive look at project management for music projects. Strong emphasis on finding a vision and mapping all work from that. The techniques are varied, from graphical strategies (Gantt charts) to refinements on brainstorming techniques. Completing projects is the overall emphasis.

Attachments
Berklee Press emblem for the top right corner

- Postcard for *Project Management for Musicians* Online Course

- *West Side Story* concert poster

- Also: See berkleepress.com for examples of our other book covers, particularly in the "New Releases" tab to see our current preferred design styles.

FIG. 44.2. Design Spec for *Project Management for Musicians* Book Cover

45. PROJECT SCOPE STATEMENT

A *project scope statement* is a document in which you store your current decisions regarding the essential parameters of your project—what you are doing and why. It begins life as a project planning document and then gets updated throughout the project's lifecycle as the project evolves. So, if you decide to do a cover song, as well as your four originals on your EP, it gets marked on the scope statement and then circulated to everyone who needs to know about that change. In this way, everyone knows exactly what the project is. When you say that you are on the same page, this is the page you are on. The scope statement tends to inform many other types of documents: business plans, contracts, budgets, and others. It is most useful if it is short and nimble and easily updated. Two to four pages long is about right. More than that, and it becomes a beast that nobody wants to deal with, rather than a helpful and informative living document. Keep it lean and mean.

Adapt this Project Scope Statement template to your project's specific needs and culture. Some options are included in the header names; choose the one that best suits your team.

[Your Project Name]
Project Scope Statement

[version date]

Summary
[A short, clear sentence or two clarifying what the project is.]

Objectives
[Why are you doing it?]

- [Three to five bullets clarifying the project's purpose. Money? More fans? Networking? Art for its own sake? A means to work independently? A supporting component for another project?]

Deliverables/Components

- [List the major components of the work—around five, or so.]

Acceptance Criteria/Success Metrics

- [Describe the criteria for success. Is there an important deadline? Quality standard? Preparedness for something? What are your metrics for the project to be considered "good?"]

Exclusions or Is/Is Not List
[Clarify what the work is and is not, particularly if there is likely confusion.]

Is:	Is Not:

Constraints
[Enter major budget items, including anticipated resources (funding you have) and expenses (costs). Attach a more detailed report, and reference it here. For "Status," indicate the funding source, or whether it is secure or not.]

Budget: See attachment.

Item	Amount	Comment	Status
Resources			
Total Resources			
Expenses			
Total Expenses			

Milestones:
[List the major important dates or points of accomplishment. In "Status," indicate whether it is started, assigned, on track, in trouble, complete, etc.]

Date	Description	Status

Assumptions
[List any parameters that you are hoping will be true, for purposes of moving forward. If they prove not to be, you need to reconsider some important dimension of the strategy. Indicate the person who will be vigilantly tracking this circumstance to determine whether action is needed.]

Item	Tracked By	Status	Mitigation Plan

Dependencies
[List any project component that relies on the completion of any other project component before it can be done.]

Stakeholders/Project Team
[List the members of your project team. For "Distribution List," indicate anyone who should receive updated copies of this scope statement, whenever there are changes made to it. If you know of a role but haven't fulfilled it yet, indicate "Needed" in the name. You might keep a simpler chart here and reference a more detailed one, such as a RASCI chart, as an attachment.]

Distribution List	Name and Contact	Roles and Responsibilities	Comment

Attachments
[List supplementary documents.]

- [Attachment A. Budget]

Version History
[List previous versions and dates, and indicate the major changes and decisions. If it's useful for you to do so.]

FIG. 45. Project Scope Statement. A free, downloadable Word template of this document (and others) can be found at www.projectmanagementformusicians.com.

46. WORK BREAKDOWN STRUCTURE

A *work breakdown structure* (WBS) is a chart showing exactly what work is required of a project. Each node (rectangle) is a *deliverable*—a component of the project that someone needs to make happen, which gets broken down and described in more detail with each generation of the tree. Ideally, the first three rows will describe 100 percent of the work. You can continue breaking it down, until it is a manageable chunk of work. (Some say the lowest level "work packet" should require eight to eighty hours of work.) At that point, instead of nouns, you can start thinking about verbs and start generating lists of the actions required to actually deliver that project component.

A WBS is a very intuitive way to view work and wrap your mind around what needs to be done. If you are doing a back-of-the-envelope plan about how a project will go, this is likely what you should draw on the back of your envelope. A common next step is to then add required time, money, or other resources to each node. Eventually, it becomes easier to switch from the graphical chart form to the more adaptable text form of the chart, which can then be turned into a chart with many more possibilities.

Here's a WBS for an album. You can see that not all nodes are fully "elaborated" by being broken down fully. Commonly, you only go into detail on what you currently want to control, particularly if the project is unstable and likely to change.

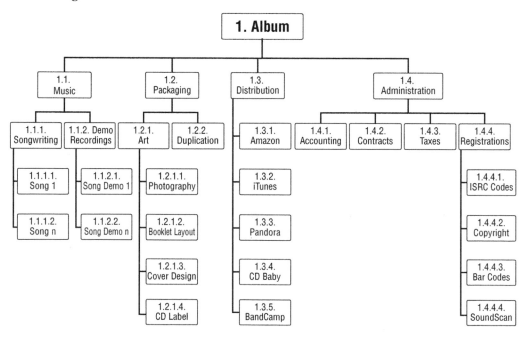

FIG. 46.1. Work Breakdown Structure for an Album

Here's the WBS in text form, focusing on the packaging portion of it. Not as intuitive to look at, but a bit more adaptable to other kinds of documents.

1. Album

    1.1. Music

    1.2. Packaging

        1.2.1. Art

            1.2.1.1. Photography

            1.2.1.2. Booklet Layout

            1.2.1.3. Cover Design

            1.2.1.4. CD Label

        1.2.2. Duplication

    1.3. Distribution

    1.4. Administration

    1.5. Project Management

FIG. 46.2. WBS for an Album: Text Form

47. TASK LIST

When it is time to actually do the work, each deliverable/component gets broken down into a *task list* (or *action list*), which is the real step-by-step nitty-gritty of what needs to happen, with additional information about each task as needed. An action list for the "Songwriting" component of this project, for example, might look like figure 47. This is a good format for getting progress reports from your staff, as well.

1.1.1. Songwriting

Action	Required Time (Days)	Assigned To	Status	Due
Go hiking to get inspiration for songs	2	Shane	Done	8/5
Write song 1	1	Shane	Done	8/6
Create voice/guitar demo of song 1	2	Shane/Rich	In progress	8/8
Send demo to band for feedback	3	Shane		8/11
Revise song 1	3	Shane/Rich		8/14
Write song 2....	1	Rich		8/15

FIG. 47. Task List for Deliverable 1.1.1. Songwriting

48. PROJECT LIST

A *project list* (or *project index* or *portfolio overview*) is a master index of all of your work. When I teach project management, one of my early class exercises is to have students list all of the projects that they feel they are currently working on, or intending to work on—every single one, whether for work or for play. They can be confronted with a list that is hundreds of projects long, which they realize is actually an impossibility. So, the next step for them is to prioritize their projects and decide what they will actually try to accomplish, based on the laws of reality and physics. It can be liberating or disheartening, but it is important to approach your work from a realistic perspective.

This is the second document I look at every morning, after my calendar. It reveals what I should be doing with my day. Because I manage about forty similar book projects simultaneously, my actual project list is a bit more elaborate than this, with columns serving as status indicators for various components of the project, so I can see at a glance what needs to happen next. The "w" in the priority column indicates that I'm waiting for someone to do something before any further progress can be made.

Priority	Project Name	Status/Most Recent Progress	Next Task	Duration (Hours)	Project Completion Date
1	Article for magazine	Received/reviewed samples.	brainstorm topics	1	6/1
2	July 4th Concert	Kass agrees to design programs but she needs final text.	decide on final program (6/4)	2	7/4
w	Pub gig	Pete says it's a go. He'll send the contract.	awaiting contract (5/28)	1	9/1
...					

FIG. 48. Project List

49. PUNCH LIST

A *punch list* is a checklist of errata, created at the end of a project—minor outstanding details that need to be addressed so that the project can conclude and everyone can get on with their lives. It can be a way of clarifying the final scope of work, so that the end game of the project doesn't go on forever. At some point, particularly when someone is asking for many generations of final changes, it makes sense to circulate (and possibly have all parties sign) a punch list. Once the items on that final list are done, then the project is over and whoever is on the hook for that component of the work can get paid. Figure 49 is a punch list for a few items outstanding in a mixing session. An engineer might create a list like this to clarify the final steps. Once it is completed and approved, the issue is settled.

It is called a "punch list" because it originated with carpenters, who would walk through a building with such a list and punch a hole next to each item with a nail, to show that it was addressed.

Complete	Issue	Approved
	1. Song 1	
	Make bass louder throughout	
	Omit "pop" at 2:04	
	2. Song 2	
	Add 1 more second between tracks 2 and 3	
	3. Song 4	
	Use take 3 of guitar solo at 1:34 to 1:54	

FIG. 49. Punch List for Mix Session

50. PROPOSAL SUMMARY

A *proposal summary* (or *project charter*) is an internal document at a record label, publishing house, investment company, etc., that organizes the essential information about a project in a standardized format. It is optimized for the review team's needs rather than the project proposer's guess at what the reviewers want to see. When a proposal is strong enough to warrant serious consideration, the acquisitions director/editor (or project manager) prepares a summary based on the proposer's submission, and updates it throughout the approval process in accordance with any decisions made about it. The person who proposed the project might not ever actually see this form.

We use the following form internally at Berklee Press to circulate and review book proposals. Different people throughout the approval process look for different elements of the proposal. Some are concerned with the genre, physical "trim" (page) size, and page count; others with the title; and others with the chapter outline's pedagogical approach. There are frequently attachments, such as the prospective author's original proposal, sample chapters, and so on. Reviewers who want to dig deeper can do so.

When projects are approved, this document is modified to become "exhibit A" of the author's contract, and then after signing, into a project scope statement.

Here's the project proposal summary (excerpted) used for this very book.

Proposal Summary

Book Name: Music Industry Forms

Author: Jonathan Feist

Date: January 7, 2013

Summary: A collection of about 70 organizational forms used in various aspects of the music industry. Each form will be annotated and have a short introduction/explanation. The research for this project will include discussions with Berklee faculty members and music industry professionals, in order to get versions of these forms that are as supportive as possible of the Berklee curriculum, as well as industry best practice.

Format: 8.5 x 11, 128 pages

Market: Wide spectrum of musicians. Would support other music business courses, and also tie into other Berklee department preferences, as possible.

Topical Outline

This is a tentative list of potential forms. Some forms are expected to come and go, as the research gets underway.

Part I. On Stage

1. Stage Plot

2. Sound Plot

3. Lighting Plot [Note that this proposed form didn't make it into the final book.]

4. Set List

[…see the table of contents for more forms…]

_____   _____
Signature, Project Review Committee Member   **Date**

_____Approved   _____Not Approved

Comments:

FIG. 50. Proposal Summary

51. JOB ASSIGNMENT MATRIX

A *job assignment matrix* is used to delegate tasks to a team of people. One like this was used in the concert halls office to organize ushers, assigning them stations and responsibilities during a concert.

Usher Stations

Date: January 9, 2013   **House Manager:** Carin

Ushers:	Emma	Lyric	Lorenzo	Sam	Annie	Craig	Beth	Rob	Porthos
Stations									
Main Entrance	P	F							
Stairs			P						
L Orchestra				P	F				
R Orchestra						F			P
Balcony							P	F	
Cleanup									
Orchestra	C	C			C				
Back Hall			C	C		C			
Balcony							C	C	C

Key: Programs, **F**lashlights, **C**leanup

FIG. 51. Usher Station Chart

52. RISK MITIGATION CHART

Risk management is the process of imagining and preparing for catastrophe (or perhaps, just inconvenience). The chart below helps articulate your planned reaction to potential hazards that might threaten a project. Each task/hazard is assigned an "owner" who is responsible for the mitigation strategies, which help prevent the hazard from occurring, and also the contingency, which is the reaction to the hazard if the unfortunate circumstance should come to pass. The Notes column can be used to fill in details as the project advances.

Task	Hazard	Level	Owner	Mitigation Strategy	Contingency	Notes
Rehearsal	Incomplete attendance	U	Sue	Reminder a week before and the day before. Get written confirmation from everyone that they will attend.	Send recording of rest of band. Have next rehearsal at the absent member's house	Bo hasn't confirmed.
Recording	Files lost due to hard drive failure	M	Bo	Back up files every night on cloud-based server (Gobbler). Burn DVD with all project files. Annually confirm that archives are OK.	We agree not to rerecord, if they are ever lost.	No offsite backup currently exists for our previous album.
Concert	Fog machine malfunctions	M	Zoë	Test the week before and the day before. Make sure we have backup fluid. Confirm stage manager has working fire extinguisher.	Don't do verse 3 if fog machine isn't working.	Checked on 11/10

FIG. 52.1. Risk Mitigation Chart for Performance

Risk Assessment Matrix

The *risk assessment matrix* is used to populate the Level column of the risk mitigation chart. To rate each risk in greater granularity and rank each in order of priority, numbers can be assigned to the Impact and Likelihood parameters, which get multiplied together. That number can be used to prioritize the most significant risks so that strategies are developed for what is most important. This chart is based on the CRM approach, developed by the U.S. Army. They found that four categories of risk were easier to work with than a numeric rating system.

RISK ASSESSMENT MATRIX		Likelihood		
		Nearly Certain	Possible	Remote
Impact	**Catastrophic**	Urgent	High	Moderate
	Significant	High	Moderate	Low
	Negligible	Moderate	Low	Low

FIG. 52.2. Risk Assessment Matrix

53. TELEPHONE TREE

A *telephone tree* (or *emergency phone tree*) is a plan for contacting a large group of people by phone. It is useful when word needs to get out quickly to a group of people that there has been a change in plans, like a concert has been cancelled due to bad weather. It is also useful for general outreach, like fundraising or organizing flash mobs. The alternative to a phone tree is that one person contacts a large number of people; a phone tree instead spreads the work around, and because calls can happen simultaneously, it is theoretically faster. Every caller gets a copy of the tree.

There are various ways to set up a phone tree. A simple way is a pyramid, where each person calls the two people below his or her name. This is a very democratic approach. For a larger group, such as attendees of a concert, a system can be set up where a team of callers each has a list of, say, ten or twenty people (non-callers) to contact, plus responsibility for contacting another caller, who also has a list.

If someone can't reach one of the people, they must take responsibility for the two people under that person's name, and when they finally reach the missing person, they can guilt trip him or her about having done their job for them. So, in this example, if Cricket can't get a hold of Barney, she has to then call Goliath and P.B., and Barney would owe her big time. The call is only considered complete if the recipient acknowledges the connection and confirms that he or she is able to continue the chain. Leaving a voice mail message doesn't count as a completed call. Without a confirmation, the caller must take responsibility for the intended recipient's calls.

Ideally, when you create a phone tree, include everyone's phone number—or several phone numbers, on the tree itself. Phone numbers are left out of this example. I mean, let's face it, some of the people referenced below actually walk on four legs. They are more likely to have dog beds or barn stall numbers than cell phones.

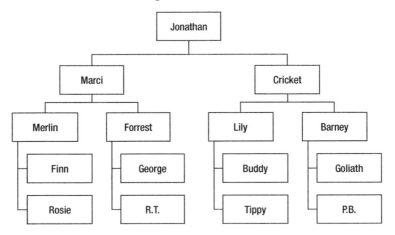

FIG. 53. Telephone Tree

54. MEETING AGENDA

An *agenda* is a schedule of what is to be covered during a meeting. By planning the meeting and scripting it out in advance, whoever is running the meeting can prioritize the business to be discussed, possibly as a result of conversation with others. Distributing it in advance lets the participants know what to cover and when important decisions will be made. It also gives them an opportunity to provide information to the leader or the group in advance of the meeting, if they want to weigh in. Agendas make meetings run more smoothly and yield more productive results. Note: Meetings of public boards, such as school committees, might legally be required to publicly post an agenda several days in advance of the meeting. Check your local open meetings law for details.

AGENDA: Tour Logistics Meeting
February 2, 2013 • 8:00 PM • At Emily's House

Topic	Duration	Decision	Attachments
1. State of the Band	10 min		
2. Confirmed Venues	20 min		Tour Stop Chart
3. Accommodations: • What do you want to pay for hotels? • Any friends nearby where we can stay for free?	25 min	x	Potential Hotels List
4. Van Repairs	10 min	x	Mechanic Assessment
5. Committee Reports	20 min		
6. What's on Your Mind?	20 min		
7. Goals for Next Month	5 min		

FIG. 54. Agenda

55. MEETING MINUTES

Meeting minutes are a record of important decisions made at the meeting. Sometimes, they continue to be important for years after the meeting occurred. Some people like to take detailed notes of what transpired during the course of the meeting. The critical information, though, is what general topics were discussed, what decisions were made, and who agreed to take responsibility for completing a task. It is also important to indicate who was present. The agenda often makes a good starting point for the minutes. As with agendas, specific laws might apply to minutes for public boards. Check your local open meetings law for details.

MINUTES: Tour Logistics Meeting
February 2, 2013 • 8:00 PM • At Emily's House

Present: Emily, Mike, David, Andrew

Absent/Late: David arrived right before the Accommodations discussion

Guest: Aaron the mix engineer

1. State of the Band
Emily updated us on timing of upcoming rehearsals and recording session (2/18).

2. Confirmed Venues
We reviewed the different stops on the upcoming tour.

3. Accommodations
We agreed to each pay up to $80 per night for our own separate rooms.

Andrew will see if his friends outside Memphis will put us up. We will all send feelers out to people we know in New Orleans, or decide to pay for hotels, by March 1.

4. Van Repairs
We agree to pay for the new brakes out of band funds but will wait to get the van detailed until after the tour.

5. Committee Reports
T-shirts will arrive by 2/21.

Aaron the engineer says that we can have the studio at a 25% discount during month of August, but we have to decide by March 15.

6. What's on Your Mind?
David thinks the website is due for an overhaul and will present a plan next month.

7. Goals for Next Month
Decide if we will be ready to do more recording by August.

Minutes by, David

FIG. 55. Minutes

56. FAQ

A *frequently asked questions* list (FAQ) is a system of common questions and answers. A clear, on-target FAQ can be a useful way to reduce confusion and risk, communicate procedures, and help everything run more efficiently. They are also a way to encourage institutional memory and make the results of extensive problem-solving efforts durable, permanently implementing them as part of operations. FAQs serve as catchalls for questions that might otherwise be difficult to organize. They might start out as a simple posted list. Sometimes, they evolve to become rules and procedures handbooks.

If the document can fit on one page, the questions and answers are featured together, simply. If it is longer, the standard format for an extended FAQ is to have the questions organized by category at the beginning, with a numeric coding system. Below that, all the questions are presented again with their answers, using the same numeric codes. This format is particularly well suited to Web pages, as the links make jumping from the questions to the answer very easy.

Here's a sample extended FAQ for concert hall operations. Just the first two categories of questions are answered here, so that you can see the numbering system at work.

Concert Hall FAQ

QUESTIONS

1. General
    1.1. Emergency Contact List
    1.2. Who has the keys?
    ...
2. Stage Manager
    2.1. When should I ring the warning buzzer?
    2.2. What needs to be done after the concert?
    ...
3. House Manager
4. Ushers
5. Building Operations
6. Performers

...

ANSWERS

1. General

   1.1. Emergency Contact List

   - Building operations: ext. 1234
   - Police/Fire/Ambulance: 911
   - House Manager: ext. 4321
   - Building Security: dial 0,0
   - Maintenance: ext. 1246

   1.2. Who has the keys?

   - Building operations (ext. 1234) has all door keys except for:
     - Sound Closet: Jack: cell number xxx-xxx-xxxx.
     - Grand Piano: Stage Manager Cabinet, black ring
     - Percussion Cabinet: Stage Manager Cabinet, gold ring
     - Green Room: Stage Manager Cabinet, green ring

2. Stage Manager

   2.1. When should I ring the warning buzzer?

   - First Ring: 10 minutes before downbeat. Confirm first with lead artist.
   - Second Ring: 3 minutes before downbeat. Before the 3-minute buzzer, contact the House Manager to confirm that he or she is ready. The house manager must signal the 3-minute warning. Inform artist.
   - Dim Lights: 30 seconds before downbeat.
   - Note: Hold the buzzer for three seconds. If it doesn't work, blink the house lights three times instead, and call Building Operations to request that it gets fixed.

   2.2. What needs to be done after the concert?

   - Sweep the stage using sweeping compound, and remove any trash.
   - Check the roster to see if a morning setup is required, and if so, do it.
   - If no morning setup is required, clear the stage completely, including chairs, stands, risers, sound equipment, instruments, and all other objects.
   - Make sure green room is broom clean.
   - Audience chairs need to be in the upright position, and any trash should be removed. Leftover programs should be recycled. (Note: The custodian will clean the audience area more thoroughly.)
   - All lights get turned off except switch 16.
   - The grand piano gets locked and covered.
   - Confirm that the piano, percussion, and green room keys are in the stage manager cabinet.
   - Fill out "Maintenance Request Form" and put it in the Building Operations mailbox, if necessary (e.g., anything that requires repair, bulbs are burned out, etc.). If anything requires immediate attention, also leave them a voicemail.
   - Lock the house doors.

3. House Manager

4. Ushers

5. Building Operations

6. Performers

...

FIG. 56. Concert Hall FAQ

PART VIII

On Campus/ At the Audition

These forms are common in music schools, lessons, and anywhere auditions are held.

57. CLASS TIMELINE AND LESSON PLAN

A *class timeline* lists the elements a teacher plans to cover or do during a lecture or period, with estimated timings for each component. It is handy to keep this visible while presenting.

Timeline

1. Review of Previous Lesson, "Blues Form"	5 minutes
2. Presentation, a "Minor Pentatonic Scale"	10 minutes
3. Live Demonstration	15 minutes
4. Workshop, "Play over Changes"	20 minutes
5. Homework Discussion	5 minutes
6. Q/A	~5 minutes

FIG. 57.1. Class Timeline

A *lesson plan* is a teacher's map for what/how to present, with reminders of the lesson objectives, materials needed, timing, overarching pedagogical purpose, and everything else to remember about the lesson. When a course is being developed, a formal plan for each lesson might be required by the school administration.

Lesson Plan

Title:	Improvising with the Major Pentatonic Scale
Time:	60 minutes
Objectives:	• Learn relationship between improvisation, song form, and scales • Learn major pentatonic scale and 12-bar blues form • Write simple solo based on major pentatonic scale • Spontaneously improvise using a major pentatonic scale
Materials:	• Play-along recording of blues form (use *Berklee Practice Method* CD tracks 8 and 12) • Lead sheets for "Do It Now" • Manuscript paper (students' notebooks)
Equipment Needed:	• Sound system (with CD player) • Keyboard • Whiteboard with staff
In-Class Workshop:	• Play blues track loop; students each get to try three choruses
Assessment Criteria:	• Are they using only the notes in the scale? • Are they organizing their solo to fit the form? • Are they keeping time? • Are they just playing the scale verbatim/mechanically, or are they creating unique patterns of notes and rhythms? • Is it musical, with care to note choices, sound, phrasing, and a narrative architecture?
Homework:	• Record solo to "Do It Now" • Challenge: Record minor pentatonic scale solo on "Leave Me Alone"

FIG. 57.2. Lesson Plan

58. GRADE BOOK

A *grade book* tracks a group of students' progress throughout a semester. This one tracks scores on assignment (A) and class participation (P), as well as a final project for each student; it should be customized to track whatever is due and whatever criteria are assessed to arrive at a final grade. The "Average" column can be kept up to date throughout the semester. This grade book is kept short, for illustration purposes, but grade books are generally oriented horizontally on a page (or two) so as to fit more detail.

Numeric scoring, as opposed to letter grades, facilitates averaging, as does using a spreadsheet program (or dedicated grade book software) to perform calculations.

The Class Average line at the bottom helps uncover systemic problems. If class after class consistently scores low on an assignment, the teacher knows to look at the teaching approach or the assessment, and consider their efficacy or how well they match.

Trombone Choir		Week 1		Week 2		Week 3		Week 4		Week 5		Week 6		Final Project	Notes
Student Name	Average	A	P	A	P	A	P	A	P	A	P	A	P		
Barney															
Buddy															
Lily															
R.T.															
George															
Josie															
Rosie															
Class Average															

FIG. 58. Grade Book. A = Assignment, P = Participation.

59. PRACTICE LOG

A *practice log* charts the time spent at different dimensions of practice. Some students will tend to over-practice within their comfort zone, so explicitly parsing it out like this can encourage more comprehensive learning to occur. Calculating weekly totals gives the student flexibility to focus more on certain dimensions on any given day, rather than forcing just a brief period on every topic every day. They can thus strive to cover all aspects of practice every week.

Timing goals (after the slash) can be pre-entered in the Total columns. Below, additional emphasis is prescribed for practicing improvisation (four hours indicated in the bottom Total field, compared to two hours for other dimensions). Sunday has yet to be entered. By keeping a running total, Lillian can tell that she's generally exceeding her goals, but that she is also coming up short for Ear Training, so she might focus there, to catch up.

Student: *Lillian*					Dates: *November 24 to 30*		
	Technique	Ear Training	Repertoire	Reading	Improv.	Ensemble	Total
Mon.	:30		1		1		2:30/2
Tues.	:15	:30	1		1		2:45/2
Wed.	:15		1		1		2:15/2
Thur.	:15	:15	1:15		:30		2:15/2
Fri.	:15	:15	:30	:30	1		2:30/2
Sat.	:15	:15	1		1	1	3:30/2
Sun.							/2
Total:	1:45/2	1:15/2	5:45/2	:30/2	5:30/4	1/2	**15:45/14**

FIG. 59. Practice Log

60. AUDITION RATING SHEET

An *audition rating sheet* is used to boil down the essential elements of an individual's audition to the most essential criteria. This sheet allows the judge to score each criteria and rate each on a weighted scale, if desired. Using this sheet, you then add the scores together to get a final rating. In addition to the usual hard skills, this audition sheet includes *x-factor*—that certain "something" that isn't covered by the scripted criteria. By systematizing this as a real-world contributing factor, you can make sure it commands an appropriate space in the decision-making process.

Bass Auditions November 10, 2013

Candidate Name/Contact Info: *Naomi Poodles*   **Jurist Name:** *Mr. Bruce*

	Score		Comment
Technique	1–15	13	Good form. Holds instrument a little low.
Improvisation	1–5	5	Imaginative, and good note choices
Stage Presence	1–5	5	Very engaging
Melodic Memory	1–5	3	
Reading	1–10	3	Needs practice here
Timing	1–20	18	
Sound	1–15	12	
X-Factor	1–25	25	Magical!
TOTAL:	Out of 100	84	Gifted! Can dance. Sign her up!

FIG. 60. Audition Rating Sheet

61. AUDITION SUMMARY MATRIX

An *audition summary matrix* can help you compress a tremendous amount of data (such as from audition rating sheets, form 60) into a matrix that you can scan at a glance. The goal here is to summarize the candidates in relationship to each other while their relative audition performances are still fresh in the jury's minds. Then, you can quickly narrow down the field of candidates. The columns for yes/no/maybe can help you overrule the average score. Sometimes, the prescribed method just doesn't cover what's needed.

When it's done, see what the data reveals. If you feel like you've got a lot of qualified candidates, the break point of where to invite people for further audition rounds could become evident, based on their exact overall score.

Essentially, you want to determine how much time you need for the next round of auditions, decide what else you need to test for, and then make some decisions.

Name	Score	Yes	No	Maybe	Comment
Lillian Athena	72	X			Solid technique. Mother is on the board.
Naomi Poodles	84	X			Great presence. Can dance.
Joshua Frogface	81			X	Good player, but has schedule conflicts. Might not be able to make it.
Howie Rott	74		X		Auditioned drunk! Reject!
...					

FIG. 61. Audition Summary Matrix

PART IX

Agreements

Agreements, whether letters of agreement or formal contracts, help clarify how your business will be conducted. Best practice is to get a music lawyer to draft these for you, rather than to use free forms from a book or from the Internet. The samples included here are intended as illustrations only, and not recommended as replacements for language that should really be crafted to your specific situation. However, these models will hopefully shed some light on a few of the common agreements you are likely to need or come across.

Again, don't let these or any samples rule your reality. Customize them to your specific situation—ideally, with the help of a competent music attorney. Be safe!

62. CO-SONGWRITER SPLIT SHEET

A *split sheet* is a simple agreement between songwriters that clarifies the percentage each owns of the writer's share of the copyright. The terms should be discussed in advance of a co-writing session, and the sheet(s) should be signed at the writing session, one for each song. Generally, songwriters tend to split copyrights evenly, no matter what each person contributed, but that's more custom than legal guideline, and bands have broken up over how much each person should own.

While songwriter egos can be complex, the split sheet itself is a simple affair—just essential names, song information, the PRO (performance rights organization) associated with each writer, and places to sign. Split sheets serve as important legal points of reference, though. While the important dimension of these agreements is the copyright ownership, they might also specify terms for how the songwriters will pay for song demos.

This is a sample split sheet. When there are likely to be large sums of money at stake, a more extended formal contract might be drafted by lawyers.

Song Title: **Date of Creation:**

Album/Project Title:

The following contributors agree to split the copyright ownership and project expenses in accordance with the indicated percentages.

Songwriter	Contact	PRO	Percentage Ownership

_____   _____
Name/Signature/Date   Name/Signature/Date

FIG. 62. Split Sheet

63. WORK-FOR-HIRE RELEASE

A *work for hire* is a type of compensation model in which someone receives a one-time payment for their efforts, as opposed to receiving ongoing royalties. Whoever creates the work for hire typically doesn't have any copyright ownership of the ultimate product. These release agreements are commonly used when hiring musicians to play on recordings. It clarifies that the person being hired relinquishes all claims on what they are helping to create, and that after the initial payment, no further compensation will be provided.

I hereby grant **[Your name]** and [his/her] legal representatives, and assigns and those acting with their authority and permission, the absolute right and permission to copyright and use, re-use, publish, and re-publish recordings of myself playing, or in which I may be included, in whole or in part in any and all media now and hereafter known, and for use as an audio product to be sold with or without music publications, or any other purpose whatsoever.

I hereby waive any right that I may have to inspect or approve the finished product or products or the advertising, promotion, printed, or other matter that may be used in connection therewith or the use to which the recording may be applied.

I hereby release, discharge, and agree to save harmless [Your name] and her legal representatives or assigns and all persons acting with their permission or authority from any liability by virtue of altering, editing, or remixing said recording, whether intentional or otherwise, that may occur or be produced in the production of said recordings or in any subsequent publications thereof.

I will be paid by **[Your name]**, a fee of **[$xxx.xx]** for my recording services. I realize I will not receive any residual payments or royalties based on the sale of the recording.

I hereby warrant that I am of full legal age and have every right to contract for the above regard. I state further that I have read the above Work-for-Hire authorization and that I am fully familiar with the contents thereof. This release shall be binding upon me and my heirs, legal representative, and assigns.

_____

Printed Name, Signature   Date

_____

Address

_____

Witness Name, Signature   Date

FIG. 63. Work-for-Hire Release. Courtesy of Debbie and Friends.

64. ANTIPIRACY CEASE AND DESIST LETTER

When you discover your songs, artwork, photos, lyrics, or other intellectual property available for free on someone else's website, the first step is to send them a *cease and desist letter*. To *cease* means that they must stop. To *desist* means that they can't do it again in the future. If this doesn't work, the next step is a stronger letter from a lawyer, and the next step after that is having them arrested.

Piracy is often conducted by unscrupulous villains who are trying to gain income through the reselling of stolen property (e.g., your songs). Sometimes, though, piracy is the work of ardent fans who are simply clueless that they are doing something illegal. So, the language and approach can be tempered here. You want to be clear that you mean business, but there are ways of presenting your case that are a little less intimidating than the following sample letter. It's important to be clear, though, regarding what the violation is and what you expect the recipient to do about it.

[Date]

Dear **[despicable pirate's name]**,

This notice is to inform you that the website **[specify the URL]** is featuring without legal authorization the following materials, to which I own the copyright:

[List of items]

This pirated, unauthorized use is illegal and in direct violation of our copyright. Whether it is you providing them personally, or your staff/clients/members working for **[company name]** is responsible, you are ultimately responsible for providing this illegal access and will be held liable unless the matter is promptly rectified.

Therefore, we demand that these materials be removed from your site immediately. If in 24 hours they are still available, or become available again in the future, I will pass this matter along to our legal department, and we will prosecute the matter vigorously. If you would like to provide us with fair compensation in return for the material's usage, we can discuss that, but the materials must come down immediately, now, until a negotiated agreement has been reached.

Signed,

[Your name]

FIG. 64. Cease and Desist Letter

65. BOOKING SHEET

A gig *booking sheet* is a simple short-form performance agreement, usually used when the money involved is relatively low. More than a couple thousand dollars, and you'll want a more substantial contract, often called a "performance agreement." Performance agreements are generally more formal contracts, and are often complex affairs. If the scope of the performance warrants it, a lawyer should draw one up.

Booking sheets are quick, easy, standard agreements that cover the essential details. For a simple one-time gig, when the resources are relatively low and the compensation is smaller than what a lawyer would cost to produce a formal contract, these short forms usually suffice.

EVENT

Event Description: Performance Date:

Artist Name: Number of Performers on Stage:

Type of Music:

SCHEDULE

Load-in Time: Length of Sets:

Sound Check Time: Length of Breaks:

Start Time: Number of Sets:

End Time:

VENUE/CONTACT DETAILS

Venue Name: Phone:

Contact Name: Cell: Email:

Address:

AGREEMENT

Venue Provides: ❑ Live Sound   ❑ Engineer   ❑ Lighting   ❑ Parking

                  ❑ Recording   ❑ Video   ❑ Merch Table   ❑ Secure Store Room

                  ❑ Advertising   ❑ Dinner/Drinks for the Band

Venue Permits: ❑ Merch Sales   ❑ Fog Machine

Total Agreed-Upon Fee: _____

Non-Refundable 50% Deposit Due 2 Weeks before Performance: _____

Balance Due: _____

Attachments: ❑ Set List   ❑ Promo Kit   ❑ Guest List (Comps)   ❑ Advertising Plan

Comments:

Cancellation Policy:

If we (the artist) must cancel the event due to matters beyond our control, such as illness, weather, act of God, electrical outage, etc., we both agree that neither of us will file any claims for damages and any monies advanced to me will be returned to you. However, if you (the venue) cancel the performance for any other reasons within 30 days of my performance, I will be compensated _____for the lost engagement. Any issues will be adjudicated under the laws of Massachusetts.

_____

Artist/Agent Name   Signature   Date

_____

Venue Contact Name   Signature   Date

FIG. 65. Booking Sheet

66. PHOTOGRAPH RELEASE

A *photograph release* (or *model release*) is an agreement granting someone the right to publish a person's image in a commercial venue, such as on an album, website, poster, and so on. The first amendment grants Americans the right to privacy, and the photo release form clarifies that the subject of the photograph gives permission for the usage intended. It must clarify the financial terms of this agreement (even if no money changes hands). If you are in the business of creating products that include photos, getting these releases as soon as someone is photographed is an important step. Many photographers keep blank forms like this onhand so that they can immediately secure a release upon taking someone's photo (such as a fan dancing in a club). Without the release, the photo will probably be commercially unusable.

Similar to the photo release is a general-purpose artwork release. If someone provides cover art for your album, they own the copyright to that art and can lay claim to a percentage of your profits, unless you work out another agreement. It is important to clarify any such usage terms before going to press.

```
Date:

For the sum of _____ and other valuable consider-
ation, receipt of which is hereby acknowledged, I hereby expressly
grant to [your company], its employees, agents, and assigns, the
right to photograph me and to use pictures, silhouettes, and other
reproductions of my physical likeness and, if [your company] so
chooses, the use of my name in connection therewith, in future
publications for [your company], and in the advertising and promo-
tion of such publications.

I hereby release and discharge [your company] from any and all
claims and demands arising out of or in connection with the use of
the photographs, including any and all claims for libel and inva-
sion of privacy. I also hereby relinquish my right to review or
approve any materials containing my likeness in advance of their
publication.

I am over the age of majority.  I have read the foregoing and
fully understand the contents thereof.

PRINTED NAME/SIGNATURE:_____ DATE:_____


ADDRESS:_____
```

FIG. 66. Photograph Release

PART X

Notation

Music notation takes many forms. What you will need depends on context, and sometimes culture. Here are a number of ways that the same music might be notated.

67. FULL SCORE

A *full score* includes full, formal notation of every part. When it's used, musicians are expected to play every note, duration, articulation, tempo marking, and so forth, precisely as written. The full score is generally used by conductors and others studying the music in its entirety, and is most common in classical music, large ensemble, film scoring, and other relatively prescriptive contexts where every note is written out.

No Time

Jonathan Feist

FIG. 67. Full Score

68. PART

A *part* excerpts the notation for a single instrument from a full score. It is used only by a specific type of instrumentalist. Here's a piano part extracted from the full score of "No Time."

No Time

Piano

Jonathan Feist

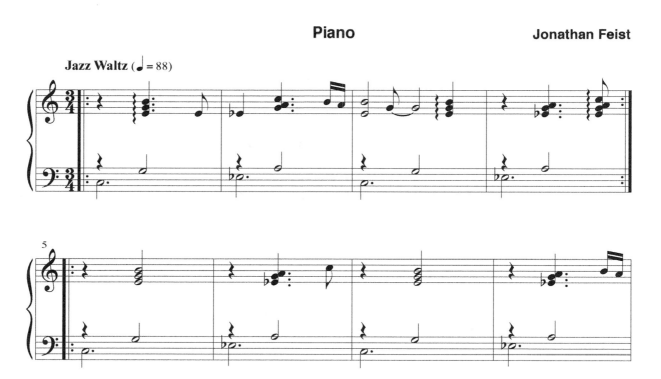

FIG. 68. Piano Part

69. PIANO/VOCAL SCORE

A *piano/vocal score* includes the vocal part and a piano accompaniment. They are sometimes distillations of larger arrangements, used for rehearsal purposes, with all instruments compressed into the piano part. Alternatively, they might be simple stand-alone arrangements. A variation of this format (common in some folk and liturgical music contexts) is to have just two piano staves, with the lyrics between them. While two staves take up less space on a page than three staves, this type of format tends to be more confusing, regarding which notes the voice should sing. (The assumption is that the vocalist sings the highest note of the voicing, which adds a creative constraint, so my own preference is for the format shown in figure 69.)

No Time

Piano/Vocal Score   **Jonathan Feist**

FIG. 69. Piano/Vocal Score

70. GUITAR TABLATURE

Tablature (or "tab" or "tabs") is notation used by fretted string instruments, such as guitar, electric bass, banjo, and others. It is particularly useful as a pedagogical tool for beginning players, though many players of all levels appreciate tab. Each line represents a string, and the numbers indicate what fret on that string is played. Tablature typically doesn't include rhythm; the expectation is that the performer knows the music and can figure out the rhythm by ear. A tablature staff might be paired with a traditional notation staff, as in figure 70. Both are read by the same, single player, who can choose whichever notation style he or she prefers. (Many guitar teachers wish that their students would learn traditional notation, while many beginning guitar students find it easiest to read tab.)

The music in figure 70 is a bit different than the full score's guitar part. It is an arrangement of "No Time" for solo guitar. (*Arrangements* are specific settings of music, generally derived from an original version.)

No Time

Jonathan Feist

FIG. 70. Guitar Traditional Notation and Tablature

71. DRUM CHART AND KEY

Drum set notation (or a *"drum chart"*) is different from notation for other instruments in that positions on the staff indicate different instruments, rather than different pitches. There are a number of competing conventions for what these positions mean. The Percussive Arts Society has codified a system that has received fairly wide acceptance among drummers, but there remain variations. Essentially, though, regular noteheads indicate drums and X noteheads indicate cymbals. Other shapes are sometimes used to indicate percussion instruments (e.g., cowbell) or special techniques (e.g., rim clicks). Stems pointing up indicate instruments played with the hands (e.g., snare drum); stems pointing down indicate instruments played with the feet (e.g., kick drum). Because drum strikes typically don't have critical duration, only attacks are usually indicated. Below, for example, the bass drum hit is notated as a dotted half note, rather than (for instance) an eighth note followed by a series of rests. Using long durations such as this greatly declutters the page.

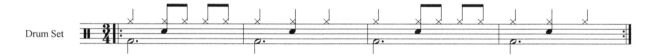

FIG. 71.1. Drum Notation

Drum Key

Drum set notation isn't universally standardized, so it is common to find a *drum key* at the beginning of a score or a book of drum notation. The key indicates exactly what conventions are being used regarding what notation character references what instrument.

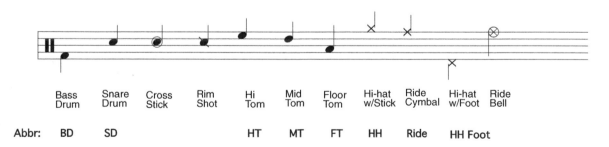

FIG. 71.2. Drum Set Key

72. LEAD SHEET

Lead sheet notation, in its purest form, includes only the melody ("lead" line) and chord symbols. Sometimes, you will also see cue notes, lyrics, rhythmic hits, and other embellishments.

Lead sheets (or "charts" or "changes") are most commonly used in jazz contexts. The notational opposite of a full score, the expectation here is that the performers will use the chart to craft their own individual parts for the tune, embellishing what is written, and developing something appropriate to their specific instruments. Every player in the band will use the same lead sheet (though a horn player might get a transposed version), but interpret the notation differently, possibly guided by the leader. A bass player, for example, will primarily look at the chord symbols (also called "changes") and craft a bass line that supports the harmonic structure. A drummer will focus on the style direction and the song form, and prepare a part that helps organize the structure. A rhythm guitarist or keyboard player would use the chord symbols to create an accompanying part ("comping") that fills in the harmonic landscape, possibly even embellishing the chord by adding "tensions" beyond what the chord symbol indicates. Collections of lead sheets are often called "fake books." In other words, a musician skilled at interpreting lead sheets can "fake" their way through playing a tune by the charts contained therein, even if they never heard the tune before.

Playing from a lead sheet probably won't result in a performance much like that achieved by the full score, but hopefully, it will have a more vibrant independent spirit. This flexibility is often puzzling to musicians who have been trained classically. But we have to get over it, somehow. Note the rhythm slashes (/ / /) in the intro; there is no melody there, just chord changes, for the groove.

No Time

Jonathan Feist

FIG. 72. Lead Sheet "No Time" Excerpt (with Lyrics)

73. CHORD CHART

A *chord chart* is like a lead sheet without the melody. Chord charts are used by rhythm section players to develop the groove accompaniment. Here is a chord chart for "No Time" (excerpt), showing just the intro and the first eight bars. The slashes in each measure indicate the beats. If we were in 4/4 time, we'd have four slashes per measure. Sometimes, the chords are written on blank paper, with no notation.

No Time

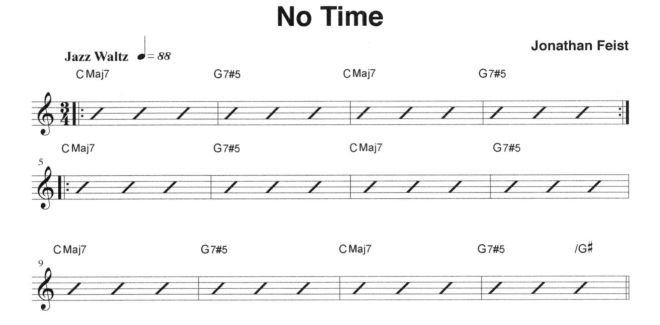

FIG. 73. Chord Chart "No Time" Excerpt

74. NASHVILLE CHORD CHART

The *Nashville numbering system* is attributed to Neil Matthews Jr. of the Jordanaires, who were best known as the backup singers for Elvis Presley, but who also worked with thousands of other artists. It is a style of chord chart, but instead of indicating specific chords, it presents chord *functions* as numerals, based on the scale (in C major, 1 for C, 2 for D, 3 for E, etc.). This facilitates transposition—common practice for session musicians who frequently adapt song keys for specific singers. A line under multiple chords indicates that they share a measure, and rhythm notation helps reveal irregular harmonic rhythms. Chord qualities beyond triads are indicated with superscripts (1^{Maj7}), or to clarify nondiatonic harmonies. You might see other symbols, such as a diamond shape to indicate "let it ring," a caret for "choke it short," slash marks (/) for chord repetitions, and others. There are many variations, with additional symbols and nuances. Essentially, though, it's a system that uses numerals instead of chord names.

Here is the Nashville-style chart for "No Time." The original jazz harmonies are a little complex for Nashville notation and would have required some finicky superscripts that would have revealed me to be the Yankee that I am, so I simplified it in order to give a more idiomatic example. For country or rock harmonies, which tend to be triadic, Nashville notation comes into its own, with simple numerals summarizing the score. It is designed to be very quick, convenient notation in a recording studio. While much detail is avoided, it provides "just enough" information to give a seasoned Nashville session musician, so that they can bang that sucker out.

This chart begins with a key and time signature: a jazz waltz in C. Thus, 1 means that the first chord here is C major, 5 means G major, 6 means A minor, and so on. If that proved too low/high for the singer and he or she decided to transpose it to, say, D major, then only one character on the chart would change (the C changing to D). Song sections, such as "intro" and "head" (once through the form) are indicated in boxes. Repeated sections don't require a restatement of the chords.

A barbeque sauce stain would make this chart more authentic. Maybe we'll add that to the upcoming scratch-'n'-sniff edition of this book.

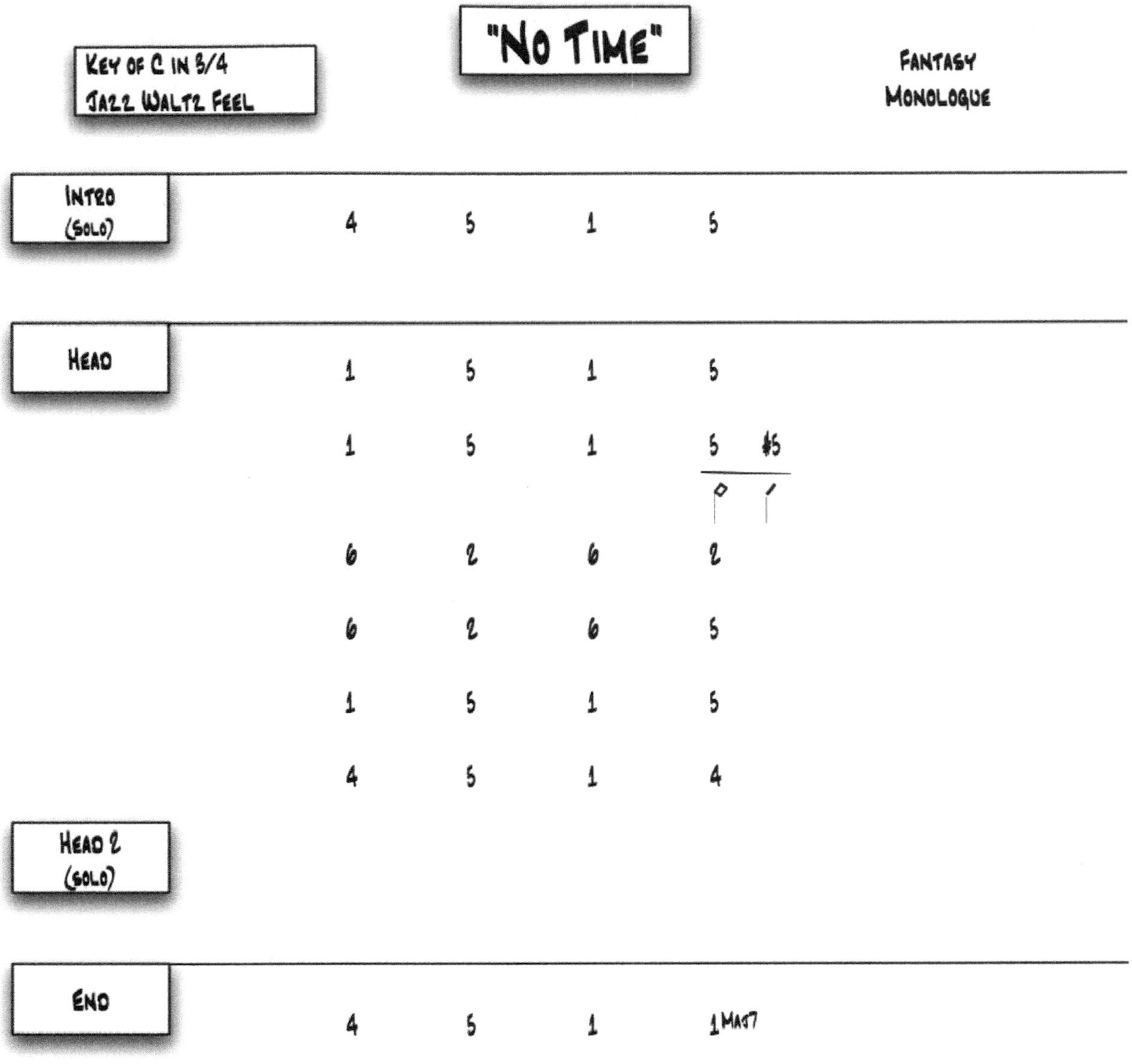

FIG. 74. Nashville Chord Chart for "No Time"

75. ARRANGEMENT SUMMARY SHEET

Accompanying a lead sheet or a set list might be a shorthand summary version of the arrangement to be performed. Whereas a set list is generally distributed to fans or to the stage manager, only performers are likely to see an arrangement summary. Song sections (verses, choruses, bridges, etc.) might be numbered, and solos indicated. The arrangement summary might be written at the bottom of a lead sheet, rather than on a separate page.

Figure 75 shows two levels of detail. For a blues, what's important is the number of measures in the form, and how many times the form is played. When everyone knows the tune, that is clear enough. For more complex forms, song sections and measure counts can be provided. The first verse of "Closet Demon," for example, is eight measures long. To confuse matters, the word "chorus" is used to mean "once through the form" for "Someone Else's Blues" (jazz style) and as a specific type of song component in "Closet Demon" (rock style).

Some common abbreviations:

H:	Head
V:	Verse
C:	Chorus
B:	Bridge
S:	Solo
Gtr.:	Guitar (and many other instrument abbreviations)
Intro:	Introduction
Out:	Out Chorus (i.e., written melody at the end)
End:	Ending/Coda

SIMPLE	DETAILED
Someone Else's Blues	**Closet Demon: D Minor**
Chorus = 12 bars	Intro: 2 bars
	V1: 8
Intro (Guitar Solo)	C1: 7
2 Choruses	V2: 8
Bridge	C2: 7
Out Chorus	V3: 8
Coda (Guitar Solo)	C3: 7
	B (Gtr. Solo): 6
	V4: 8
	C4: 6
	End (vamp): 8+

FIG. 75. Arrangement Summary

AFTERWORD. TIPS FOR CREATING FORMS

Hopefully, this collection of forms gives you some ideas for how to organize your work in the music industry. Again, they are designed to be customized to your own circumstances, rather than used verbatim.

If you see a cryptic form out there in the field, see if you can find someone to interpret it for you. Send it to me, if you like (at jfeist@berklee.edu). I live for this stuff, especially when it helps forge order out of chaos. Which begs the question, what's the difference between a good, helpful form and a torturous implement of inane bureaucracy?

Forms are communication tools, and the best forms serve a community of folks: those gathering the information, filling in the information, and interpreting the information. Bad forms commonly only represent the perspective of their creators—and sometimes, not even them. A classic mistake is to have fields so small, it is impossible for anyone to legibly fill in the required information. The form must serve the person filling it out, as well as the person reading it and creating it—even if all three roles are played by you. Thinking it through this carefully, from a general usability and communication perspective, is often half the journey towards getting it right.

Here are a few tips for creating useful, lovable forms.

1. *Keep it clear and concise.* Use standard formats, symbols, and terminologies; see if a standard exists before inventing your own. If anyone is likely to read the form who is not familiar with its conventions, include a legend of symbols, or even an attached explanation sheet. Don't set the font size so small that nobody can read it; smaller than 8 points, and you're looking for trouble. Use as little text as possible, and omit unnecessary punctuation (such as colons in headers). Be ruthless in cutting out anything unnecessary. If possible, engage a graphic designer to fine-tune the layout and help clarify the form's organization. (Junking up the form with nonessential graphics is counterproductive, though, no matter how zippy they look.)

2. *Encourage good data input.* Give enough space to handwrite information if typing it isn't possible. Make text labels as concise and understandable as you can. Using check boxes and radio buttons instead of open fields can speed up the user's data entry time and avoid confusion in their reply due to illegible handwriting or typos. Invite your form's user(s) to attach sheets of more information, if their answers could exceed the prescribed space available.

3. *Encourage completeness while avoiding excess.* Consider whether every data point is truly relevant/necessary/actionable. If not, take it off the form. If you are unlikely to actually use someone's fax number, don't request it. People lose steam when filling out information, and the quality of their input can decline as they grow fed up with a lengthy process. Just ask for what's critical.

4. *Test it before it goes live.* Ask someone to fill it out, and then evaluate how well their work suits your needs. If what they produce is difficult to read or is incomplete, make some adjustments.

5. *Simplify the user's experience.* Avoid having them go on wild goose chases or having to struggle with awkwardness. A common example is on computerized data entry fields where you have to choose your country by scrolling down a loooong list of every country on earth before arriving at "United States," all the way at the end of the alphabet. If nearly everyone who fills out the form is from the same country, you can save your population of form users a lot of collective mousing around by making that country the default. For collections of fields like components of a mailing address (City, State, Zip), set the related fields together, such as on a horizontal line, logically grouped, to match how people intuitively organize the information. And if a form is likely to be referenced by a certain name or title or code number, set that right at the top, large and unobscured, so that it is easily spotted right away. Don't surround it with junk.

I really hope that these samples and explanations make your life and work easier and help facilitate your music-making process.

And thank you for participating in the music industry. It's not always easy, but we really need you here.

ABOUT THE AUTHOR

Jonathan Feist has worked in many dimensions of the music industry, from stage manager to songwriter, producer to performer, engraver to educator. He is editor in chief of Berklee Press, the book/instructional video publishing division of Berklee College of Music (in partnership with Hal Leonard Corp.), where since 1998 he has helped bring hundreds of pedagogical music products to a worldwide audience. Jonathan is author of the book *Project Management for Musicians* and two Berklee Online courses: *Project Management for Musicians* and *Music Notation Using Finale.* He holds a bachelor's and master's degree in composition from New England Conservatory of Music.

More Fine Publications

Berklee Press

GUITAR

BEBOP GUITAR SOLOS
by Michael Kaplan
00121703 Book $16.99

BLUES GUITAR TECHNIQUE
by Michael Williams
50449623 Book/Online Audio $24.99

BERKLEE GUITAR CHORD DICTIONARY
by Rick Peckham
50449546 Jazz - Book $12.99
50449596 Rock - Book $12.99

BERKLEE GUITAR STYLE STUDIES
by Jim Kelly
00200377 Book/Online Media $24.99

CLASSICAL TECHNIQUE FOR THE MODERN GUITARIST
by Kim Perlak
00148781 Book/Online Audio $19.99

CONTEMPORARY JAZZ GUITAR SOLOS
by Michael Kaplan
00143596 Book $16.99

CREATIVE CHORDAL HARMONY FOR GUITAR
by Mick Goodrick and Tim Miller
50449613 Book/Online Audio $19.99

FUNK/R&B GUITAR
by Thaddeus Hogarth
50449569 Book/Online Audio $19.99

GUITAR SWEEP PICKING
by Joe Stump
00151223 Book/Online Audio $19.99

INTRODUCTION TO JAZZ GUITAR
by Jane Miller
00125041 Book/Online Audio $19.99

JAZZ GUITAR FRETBOARD NAVIGATION
by Mark White
00154107 Book/Online Audio $19.99

JAZZ SWING GUITAR
by Jon Wheatley
00139935 Book/Online Audio $19.99

METAL GUITAR CHOP SHOP
by Joe Stump
50449601 Book/Online Audio $19.99

A MODERN METHOD FOR GUITAR – VOLUMES 1-3 COMPLETE*
by William Leavitt
00292990 Book/Online Media $49.99
*Individual volumes, media options, and supporting songbooks available.

A MODERN METHOD FOR GUITAR SCALES
by Larry Baione
00199318 Book $10.99

READING STUDIES FOR GUITAR
by William Leavitt
50449490 Book $16.99

Berklee Press publications feature material developed at the Berklee College of Music. To browse the complete Berklee Press Catalog, go to
www.berkleepress.com

BASS

BERKLEE JAZZ BASS
by Rich Appleman, Whit Browne & Bruce Gertz
50449636 Book/Online Audio $19.99

CHORD STUDIES FOR ELECTRIC BASS
by Rich Appleman & Joseph Viola
50449750 Book $17.99

FINGERSTYLE FUNK BASS LINES
by Joe Santerre
50449542 Book/Online Audio $19.99

FUNK BASS FILLS
by Anthony Vitti
50449608 Book/Online Audio $19.99

INSTANT BASS
by Danny Morris
50449502 Book/CD $9.99

METAL BASS LINES
by David Marvuglio
00122465 Book/Online Audio $19.99

READING CONTEMPORARY ELECTRIC BASS
by Rich Appleman
50449770 Book $19.99

ROCK BASS LINES
by Joe Santerre
50449478 Book/Online Audio $22.99

PIANO/KEYBOARD

BERKLEE JAZZ KEYBOARD HARMONY
by Suzanna Sifter
00138874 Book/Online Audio $24.99

BERKLEE JAZZ PIANO
by Ray Santisi
50448047 Book/Online Audio $19.99

BERKLEE JAZZ STANDARDS FOR SOLO PIANO
arr. Robert Christopherson, Hey Rim Jeon, Ross Ramsay, Tim Ray
00160482 Book/Online Audio $19.99

CHORD-SCALE IMPROVISATION FOR KEYBOARD
by Ross Ramsay
50449597 Book/CD $19.99

CONTEMPORARY PIANO TECHNIQUE
by Stephany Tiernan
50449545 Book/DVD $29.99

HAMMOND ORGAN COMPLETE
by Dave Limina
00237801 Book/Online Audio $24.99

JAZZ PIANO COMPING
by Suzanne Davis
50449614 Book/Online Audio $19.99

LATIN JAZZ PIANO IMPROVISATION
by Rebecca Cline
50449649 Book/Online Audio $24.99

PIANO ESSENTIALS
by Ross Ramsay
50448046 Book/Online Audio $24.99

SOLO JAZZ PIANO
by Neil Olmstead
50449641 Book/Online Audio $39.99

DRUMS

BEGINNING DJEMBE
by Michael Markus & Joe Galeota
00148210 Book/Online Video $16.99

BERKLEE JAZZ DRUMS
by Casey Scheuerell
50449612 Book/Online Audio $19.99

DRUM SET WARM-UPS
by Rod Morgenstein
50449465 Book $12.99

A MANUAL FOR THE MODERN DRUMMER
by Alan Dawson & Don DeMichael
50449560 Book $14.99

MASTERING THE ART OF BRUSHES
by Jon Hazilla
50449459 Book/Online Audio $19.99

PHRASING
by Russ Gold
00120209 Book/Online Media $19.99

WORLD JAZZ DRUMMING
by Mark Walker
50449568 Book/CD $22.99

BERKLEE PRACTICE METHOD

GET YOUR BAND TOGETHER
With additional volumes for other instruments, plus a teacher's guide.
Bass
by Rich Appleman, John Repucci and the Berklee Faculty
50449427 Book/CD $19.99
Drum Set
by Ron Savage, Casey Scheuerell and the Berklee Faculty
50449429 Book/CD $14.95
Guitar
by Larry Baione and the Berklee Faculty
50449426 Book/CD $19.99
Keyboard
by Russell Hoffmann, Paul Schmeling and the Berklee Faculty
50449428 Book/Online Audio $14.99

VOICE

BELTING
by Jeannie Gagné
00124984 Book/Online Media $19.99

THE CONTEMPORARY SINGER
by Anne Peckham
50449595 Book/Online Audio $24.99

JAZZ VOCAL IMPROVISATION
by Mili Bermejo
00159290 Book/Online Audio $19.99

TIPS FOR SINGERS
by Carolyn Wilkins
50449557 Book/CD $19.95

VOCAL WORKOUTS FOR THE CONTEMPORARY SINGER
by Anne Peckham
50448044 Book/Online Audio $24.99

YOUR SINGING VOICE
by Jeannie Gagné
50449619 Book/Online Audio $29.99

WOODWINDS & BRASS

TRUMPET SOUND EFFECTS
by Craig Pederson & Ueli Dörig
00121626 Book/Online Audio............ $14.99

SAXOPHONE SOUND EFFECTS
by Ueli Dörig
50449628 Book/Online Audio.......... $15.99

THE TECHNIQUE OF THE FLUTE
by Joseph Viola
00214012 Book.................................. $19.99

STRINGS/ROOTS MUSIC

BERKLEE HARP
by Felice Pomeranz
00144263 Book/Online Audio.......... $19.99

BEYOND BLUEGRASS BANJO
by Dave Hollander and Matt Glaser
50449610 Book/CD............................ $19.99

BEYOND BLUEGRASS MANDOLIN
by John McGann and Matt Glaser
50449609 Book/CD............................ $19.99

BLUEGRASS FIDDLE & BEYOND
by Matt Glaser
50449602 Book/CD............................ $19.99

CONTEMPORARY CELLO ETUDES
by Mike Block
00159292 Book/Online Audio.......... $19.99

EXPLORING CLASSICAL MANDOLIN
by August Watters
00125040 Book/Online Media......... $22.99

THE IRISH CELLO BOOK
by Liz Davis Maxfield
50449652 Book/Online Audio......... $24.99

JAZZ UKULELE
by Abe Lagrimas, Jr.
00121624 Book/Online Audio........... $19.99

AUTOBIOGRAPHY

LEARNING TO LISTEN: THE JAZZ JOURNEY OF GARY BURTON
by Gary Burton
00117798 Book.................................. $27.99

MUSIC THEORY, EAR TRAINING & IMPROVISATION

BEGINNING EAR TRAINING
by Gilson Schachnik
50449548 Book/Online Audio.......... $16.99

BERKLEE BOOK OF JAZZ HARMONY
by Joe Mulholland & Tom Hojnacki
00113755 Book/Online Audio........... $27.50

BERKLEE MUSIC THEORY
by Paul Schmeling
50449615 Book 1/Online Audio....... $24.99
50449616 Book 2/Online Audio...... $22.99

CONTEMPORARY COUNTERPOINT
by Beth Denisch
00147050 Book/Online Audio......... $22.99

IMPROVISATION FOR CLASSICAL MUSICIANS
by Eugene Friesen with Wendy M. Friesen
50449637 Book/CD............................ $24.99

REHARMONIZATION TECHNIQUES
by Randy Felts
50449496 Book.................................. $29.99

MUSIC BUSINESS

CROWDFUNDING FOR MUSICIANS
by Laser Malena-Webber
00285092 Book.................................. $17.99

ENGAGING THE CONCERT AUDIENCE
by David Wallace
00244532 Book/Online Media.......... $16.99

HOW TO GET A JOB IN THE MUSIC INDUSTRY
by Keith Hatschek with Breanne Beseda
00130699 Book.................................. $27.99

MAKING MUSIC MAKE MONEY
by Eric Beall
50448009 Book.................................. $29.99

MUSIC INDUSTRY FORMS
by Jonathan Feist
00121814 Book.................................. $15.99

MUSIC LAW IN THE DIGITAL AGE
by Allen Bargfrede
00148196 Book.................................. $19.99

MUSIC MARKETING
by Mike King
50449588 Book.................................. $24.99

PROJECT MANAGEMENT FOR MUSICIANS
by Jonathan Feist
50449659 Book.................................. $29.99

THE SELF-PROMOTING MUSICIAN
by Peter Spellman
00119607 Book.................................. $24.99

MUSIC PRODUCTION & ENGINEERING

AUDIO MASTERING
by Jonathan Wyner
50449581 Book/CD............................ $29.99

AUDIO POST PRODUCTION
by Mark Cross
50449627 Book.................................. $19.99

CREATING COMMERCIAL MUSIC
by Peter Bell
00278535 Book/Online Media.......... $19.99

THE SINGER-SONGWRITER'S GUIDE TO RECORDING IN THE HOME STUDIO
by Shane Adams
00148211 Book.................................. $16.99

UNDERSTANDING AUDIO
by Daniel M. Thompson
00148197 Book.................................. $34.99

WELLNESS

MANAGE YOUR STRESS AND PAIN THROUGH MUSIC
by Dr. Suzanne B. Hanser and Dr. Susan E. Mandel
50449592 Book/CD $29.99

MUSICIAN'S YOGA
by Mia Olson
50449587 Book.................................. $19.99

THE NEW MUSIC THERAPIST'S HANDBOOK
by Dr. Suzanne B. Hanser
00279325 Book.................................. $29.99

Prices subject to change without notice. Visit your local music dealer or bookstore, or go to **www.berkleepress.com**

SONGWRITING, COMPOSING, ARRANGING & CONDUCTING

ARRANGING FOR HORNS
by Jerry Gates
00121625 Book/Online Audio........... $19.99

BEGINNING SONGWRITING
by Andrea Stolpe with Jan Stolpe
00138503 Book/Online Audio........... $19.99

BERKLEE CONTEMPORARY MUSIC NOTATION
by Jonathan Feist
00202547 Book.................................. $19.99

COMPLETE GUIDE TO FILM SCORING
by Richard Davis
50449607 Book.................................. $29.99

CONDUCTING MUSIC TODAY
by Bruce Hangen
00237719 Book/Online Media.......... $24.99

CONTEMPORARY COUNTERPOINT: THEORY & APPLICATION
by Beth Denisch
00147050 Book/Online Audio......... $22.99

THE CRAFT OF SONGWRITING
by Scarlet Keys
00159283 Book/Online Audio.......... $19.99

CREATIVE STRATEGIES IN FILM SCORING
by Ben Newhouse
00242911 Book/Online Media.......... $24.99

JAZZ COMPOSITION
by Ted Pease
50448000 Book/Online Audio $39.99

MELODY IN SONGWRITING
by Jack Perricone
50449419 Book.................................. $24.99

MODERN JAZZ VOICINGS
by Ted Pease and Ken Pullig
50449485 Book/Online Audio......... $24.99

MUSIC COMPOSITION FOR FILM AND TELEVISION
by Lalo Schifrin
50449604 Book.................................. $34.99

MUSIC NOTATION
by Mark McGrain
50449399 Book.................................. $24.99
by Matthew Nicholl and Richard Grudzinski
50449540 Book.................................. $19.99

POPULAR LYRIC WRITING
by Andrea Stolpe
50449553 Book.................................. $15.99

THE SONGWRITER'S WORKSHOP
by Jimmy Kachulis
Harmony
50449519 Book/Online Audio $29.99
Melody
50449518 Book/Online Audio $24.99

SONGWRITING: ESSENTIAL GUIDE
by Pat Pattison
Lyric and Form Structure
50481582 Book.................................. $16.99
Rhyming
00124366 Book.................................. $17.99

SONGWRITING IN PRACTICE
by Mark Simos
00244545 Book.................................. $16.99

SONGWRITING STRATEGIES
by Mark Simos
50449621 Book.................................. $24.99

STUDY PROJECT MANAGEMENT
with
■ BERKLEE ONLINE

Study Berklee's curriculum, with Berklee faculty members, in a collaborative online community. Transform your skill set and find your inspiration in all areas of music, from project management and music business to songwriting and music production, theory, orchestration, and everything in between. Build lifelong relationships with like-minded students on your own time, from anywhere in the world.

Discover Your Own Path At
ONLINE.BERKLEE.EDU